The Murphy's Story

The Murphy's Story
The History of Lady's Well Brewery, Cork

Diarmuid Ó Drisceoil and Donal Ó Drisceoil

British Library Cataloguing in Publication Data
A CIP catalogue record for this book is available from the British Library

First published in 1997 by Murphy Brewery Ireland Ltd.

© Diarmuid Ó Drisceoil and Donal Ó Drisceoil 1997

ISBN 0 9531431 0 4
Designed and Typeset by Kunnert and Tierney Design Consultants, Cork, Ireland
Printed by City Print, Cork, Ireland
Trade distribution by Mercier Press Ltd., P.O. Box 5, 5 French Church Street, Cork, Ireland.

Contents

Preface

This book is the story of Murphy's, the story of a brewery, its stout and its people. Murphy's has been brewed at the same Cork site since 1856 and has now become an international brand, recognised across the world.

The brothers who established James J. Murphy & Co. and Lady's Well Brewery came from one of Cork's original 'merchant prince' families, which had grown rich during the city's economic heyday in the late eighteenth and early nineteenth centuries. The brewery grew rapidly to become an established name in Irish brewing and an integral part of the physical, economic and social landscape of Cork. It continued to trade throughout the upheavals of twentieth-century Irish and international history, and has survived as a symbol of continuity in a rapidly changing world.

The Murphy's Story is a business history, but it is much more besides. It incorporates local, labour, social and cultural history and is told against the backdrop of the political and economic history of Ireland across two centuries. Many of the illustrations have never been previously published and these, together with a number of specially commissioned photographs and some more familiar images, help to illuminate a fascinating tale.

The book is intended to appeal to as wide a readership as possible; it is extensively illustrated while special highlighted pieces focus on various aspects of the history of Cork, the Murphy family and the brewery. These can be read either in isolation or in conjunction with the main narrative. To make this work as accessible and enjoyable as possible, academic conventions, such as footnotes, have not been used. However, every effort has been made to maintain historical accuracy and a scholarly standard.

A large number of people helped to make this book possible in a wide variety of ways. They gave interviews; supplied photographs, illustrations and other source materials; pointed us in particular directions; read drafts and made helpful suggestions; organised contacts and meetings, etc. We would like to acknowledge their contributions, whether large or small, and record our gratitude to them all.

Firstly, thanks to Patrick Conway, Marketing Director of Murphy Brewery Ireland Ltd (MBIL), who instigated the project and maintained a keen personal interest in it throughout. Thanks also to Marien Kakebeeke, Managing Director of MBIL, the General Management team and everybody at the brewery, in all departments, who were ever helpful and courteous. Special thanks to Jerry Quirke at reception for his friendly co-operation at all times.

We are also grateful to the following: Rex Archer, Seán Beecher, Andy Bielenberg, Gerry Burgoyne (AIB), Frank Casey, Wally Cogan, Anne Cullimore, J. J. Cronin, Tim Crowley, Christy Daly, Peter Daly, Frank Dillon, Gerald Donovan of West Cork Bottling, Pat Earley, the late Vince Giltinan, Frank Halbert, William

Harrington, Con Harrington, Donal Hosford, Tommy Hosford, Jim Hurley, Bob Kennefick, Úna Kennefick, all at Kunnert and Tierney, Denis Lenihan, Patricia Lindsell, Bernadette McCarthy, Helen McDonnell, Christopher Murphy, Jackie Murphy, Michael Murphy, Ronald P. Murphy, Diarmuid Ó Catháin, Michael O'Callaghan, Eileen O'Carroll, Tim O'Connell, Rory O'Connor, Des O'Driscoll at the *Examiner*, Thomas O'Driscoll, Colman O'Mahony, Mary Rose O'Neill, Tom O'Reilly, Charles O'Sullivan, Maura O'Sullivan, Ted O'Sullivan, Vincent and Joan O'Sullivan, Nicholas Redman, Frank Roche, Joseph G. Scroope, Jack Sheedy, Charles Thornhill, John Tobin, Mary Walsh and Noel Walsh.

We would like to thank the institutions which facilitated our research, particularly the Cork Archives Institute, Cork City Library, Cork County Library, Examiner Publications, the National Library of Ireland, Trinity College Dublin Library, University College Cork's Boole Library and the Whitbread Archive. Thanks also to the proprietors of the following Cork pubs who provided materials or allowed photographs to be taken of and on their premises: Cissie Young's, Deanrock House, The Idle Hour, Le Chateau, The Lobby, The Lough Tavern, The Outpost, The Ovens Tavern, and The Tower Inn.

Finally, a special thank you to our respective families - Miriam, Méabh and Aonghus, and Orla, Kim and Fionn - for tolerating our absences and for their patience and support. Hopefully it was all worthwhile.

Diarmuid Ó Drisceoil & Donal Ó Drisceoil,
Cork, 1997.

We are grateful to the people and organizations listed below for photographs used throughout the book:

pages 8 (right), 40, 67, 73, 87 (left), 90, 91, 96 (right), 108, 117, 129 (right), 136 (left) and 143 (second, third and fourth from the top):
The Examiner
pages 104, 111, 113 and 116: Denis Lenihan
pages x, 4 and 26: Crawford Gallery, Cork
pages 3, 7 and 8 (top left): Davison & Associates Ltd.
pages 35 and 41: Lawrence Collection, National Library of Ireland
page 7: R.P. Murphy
page 9: Patricia Lindsell
page 14: Gerry Burgoyne (AIB)
page 17: AKG Photo, London
page 22: Bridgeman Art Library

page 23: Guinness
page 72: Trinity College, Dublin
pages 74: Imperial War Museum, London
pages 77: Hulton Getty Picture Collection
page 85: National Museum of Ireland
page 96 (left): Rory O'Connor
page 97: Frank Dillon
page 106: Frank Casey
page 112: Michael O'Callaghan
page 121: William Harrington
page 129 (left): Peter Barry

Original photography by Andrew Bradley Photography and John Sheehan Photography.

MURPHYS

BREWERS

CORK

1

The Murphy Family

The Murphy brothers, who founded James J. Murphy & Co. at Lady's Well Brewery in 1856, belonged to a wealthy and distinguished Cork family that had become part of a Catholic ascendancy in commercial and industrial concerns in the city in the late eighteenth and early nineteenth centuries. The Murphy family grew powerful and prosperous through a variety of business ventures, including tea-importing, tanning, distilling and ship-owning. They had extensive economic, social and political influence in Cork city which arose, according to an account from the 1840s, 'from their great number, wealth, perfect union among themselves, and the various branches of trade in which they have nearly a monopoly'.

Origins

Family tradition tells that a Nicholas O'Murphy, who died in 1743, moved from County Kilkenny or County Laois to settle near Carrigrohane, west of Cork city, some time between 1709 and 1711, where he leased some land. In 1756 the family lost possession of the land as a result of the Penal Laws. This legislation restricted Catholic land ownership and leasing and blocked Catholics from advancement in public life but did not stop them amassing wealth in trade and industry. The dispossessed man was Jeremiah Murphy, and was probably the son of Nicholas. Jeremiah leased land also, at Bishopstown on the western side of the city. He married Mary Anne Kedmond, said to have been the only child of a

Danish soldier who settled in Ireland, and they had two sons, Daniel and Jeremiah.

Daniel Murphy, the eldest son, became a farmer and lived at Rock Farm, in the vicinity of Carrigrohane. His younger brother, Jeremiah, was born around 1746. He was put to trade as a leather worker and lived in a house on the corner of Goulnaspurra, the junction of Blarney Street and Shandon Street, then called Blarney and Mallow lanes, on the north side of the city. This area was also called Broguemakers' Hill, marking its long association with the leather trade. As Jeremiah's circumstances improved he moved from there to Barrack Street and finally to South Main Street. He married Mary Hallinan (called Hallahan or O'Halloran in some sources) around 1767. They had five sons and one daughter: James in 1769, John in 1772, Mary Anne in 1778, Jeremiah in 1779, Daniel in 1780 and Nicholas in 1785.

Jeremiah Murphy's success in the leather trade in the final decades of the eighteenth century coincided with the growth of Cork as an important tanning centre. The local population was growing rapidly, creating a demand for shoe leather, and prices doubled during this period. Tanning became the principal branch of manufacturing in the city; by the early 1800s there were forty-four tanyards employing 427 people. Jeremiah's success in his trade made him a man of some importance; when he died in 1802 his obituary stated that he was 'a man of great integrity who placed by industry a large family

1

in comfort and affluence, and died universally respected'.

The Family of Jeremiah Murphy (1746-1802)

Jeremiah Murphy's children did not squander the 'affluence' in which they were placed by their father, but rather consolidated and increased it. Katherine Donovan, a great-grandchild of

Jeremiah, tells that he made over his business to his eldest son James who 'realised an immense fortune during the Peninsular war' (1808-13), when the British and French armies fought each other for control of Spain and Portugal. One of the more extensive tanyards in Cork belonged to Daniel, fourth son of Jeremiah, and brother of James. This was located in Blackpool on the north side of the city. The firm of Daniel Murphy and Sons was not affected by the decline which ruined many tanning enterprises following the mid-1830s. A partnership formed with the firm of

Dunn Brothers maintained the business and the new firm became the largest tanning concern in the country at the time.

Jeremiah's second son, John Murphy (see highlight, p. 3), was born in 1772. He did not make a career in business but was ordained a Catholic priest in 1794. In 1815 he became Bishop of Cork, a position he held until his death in 1847. He was educated in France and Portugal. This was not unusual, as it was the habit of the wealthy Catholic merchants to send their children abroad to be educated, and fluent French was the hallmark of the class.

The other four sons (Jeremiah, Daniel, Nicholas and James), were the merchants and businessmen of the family and they profited from the great level of trade that Cork was then enjoying. They owned ships and traded as far afield as the Americas and the Far East in goods such as sugar, pepper, candy, East India indigo, Jamaica rum, Russian bar iron, coffee and tea. The latter, which was an expensive luxury at the beginning of the nineteenth century, fetched a very high price in Ireland and England. The Murphys, from their base at Morrison's Island, one of the main islands between the channels of the River Lee, ran a very lucrative tea-importing business. One of their ships was the *Jumma*, the first to trade directly between Cork and Canton in China. With their profits they bought property, including a number of fine houses in areas favoured by the wealthy on the outskirts of the city, such as Montenotte, Glanmire and Blackrock.

In 1825 James and his brothers bought a premises in Midleton, about fifteen miles east of Cork, and established a distillery, James Murphy

Left: The Murphy Family vault at Carrigrohane cemetery, near Cork city.

Above: Keys of the Murphy vault, kept at Lady's Well Brewery.

'A Book-Loving Irish Bishop'
BISHOP JOHN MURPHY

John Murphy (1772-1847) was a brother of the founders of James Murphy and Co. distillery and a granduncle of James J. Murphy and his brothers who founded the Lady's Well Brewery. He began his studies in Cork and at the age of fifteen left for Paris to begin preparing for the priesthood. While there he witnessed the outbreak of the French Revolution in 1789, an event which forced him to return home in that year. In 1791 John left Cork again to take up study at the Irish College in Lisbon, where he was ordained a priest in 1794. He returned to Cork in 1797 to become first a curate and later parish priest in the Middle Parish (SS Peter and Paul). In 1815 he was consecrated Catholic Bishop of Cork.

In his time as bishop, John Murphy oversaw the building of a number of churches and seminaries, the growth of the Ursuline and Presentation orders of nuns, and the establishment of the Sisters of Mercy and Charity in his dioceses. He was the first patron of John Hogan, the famous Cork neo-classical sculptor, a number of whose works decorated the North Chapel, as Cork's Catholic Cathedral is known. The bishop was

Bust of Bishop John Murphy (1772-1847) by John Hogan.

also instrumental in the establishment of the Cork Savings Bank in 1817, another example of the Murphy family's close association with banking in the city.

He was bishop during the first decade of Cork priest Father Theobald Mathew's famous temperance campaign, but, coming from a family of distillers, was less than enthusiastic in his support for the movement!

Bishop John Murphy is probably most famous as a book lover and collector. Thomas Davis, the writer and leading nationalist, described him colourfully as a 'glorious hearty Johnsonian bookworm'. His extensive collection (upwards of 70,000 volumes), particularly valuable for its Irish books and manuscripts, was the largest ever formed in Ireland by a private individual. His whole house was turned into a library, with books lining every wall. He wished to bequeath his library to the people of Cork, but, unfortunately, no suitable building was procured. Following the bishop's death in 1847, 120 of his volumes of Irish manuscripts were deposited in Maynooth College library by the executors of his will, but most of the collection was disposed of by auction at Sotheby's in London. It was so large that the auction was spread over an entire year. What the auctioneer described as an 'extraordinarily extensive and valuable library' of old and rare books was sold off for a fraction of its worth, and both Cork and Ireland suffered the 'irreparable loss' of an irreplaceable collection.

CORK IN THE LATE EIGHTEENTH AND EARLY NINETEENTH CENTURIES

'Paddle steamer entering the port of Cork', by George Wheatly Atkinson (1806-1884).

During the second half of the 1700s the city of Cork experienced great growth in population and economic importance. In that century the population rose from 16,000 to over 60,000. Cork became a major port and thrived through provisioning ships and exporting huge quantities of butter, beef and textiles. Until 1782 Cork was a leading centre for provisioning British navy and army supply ships and had built up a world-wide export trade based on its strategic location for ships employed in the Atlantic trade. The British army and navy had a significant presence in the city and county and this created an added demand for many of the commodities produced locally. These included gunpowder, textiles for uniforms, leather for footwear and saddlery, as well as flour, meat, spirits and beer. The city and its harbour had important shipbuilding and repair yards, in addition to glass, paper, iron and engineering works. Trade flourished and was greatly boosted during Britain's involvement in the Napoleonic Wars (1793-1815), when there was an increased demand for many products.

Many opportunities were created for the enterprising risk-taker and the lucky ones created fortunes for themselves and their families. It was at this time that many of the 'merchant princes' of the city, as they came to be known, established their dynasties, and the Murphys were among the most prominent of these.

The 'boom years' for Cork ended in the 1820s and 1830s. The dispersal of the British navy and the collapse of British military demand following the ending of the Napoleonic Wars, combined with general economic depression and the onset of British competition, had a devastating impact on the city. Manufacturing was almost wiped out but the Murphys survived and prospered because of their involvement in trade, which was less affected, and in industries which survived the slump: tanning, distilling and, later, brewing.

Right: Newspaper
advertisement
c.1820 for the firm
of James, Nicholas
and Jeremiah
Murphy.

and Co., at a cost of £30,000. This money, a vast sum for the time, came from their own resources. The enterprise rapidly became a success; in 1837 it produced 300,000 gallons of whiskey, rising to 400,000 gallons in 1850 when it employed nearly 200 people. The success of the distillery and the other family business interests secured for the Murphy family an influential place in the economic life of the city.

James Murphy (1769-1855) lived initially at Morrison's Island, but moved to Ringmahon Castle near Blackrock on the east of the city in 1818. He married Mary Gallwey (or Galwey) around 1790 and they had twelve children. The eldest of these was Jeremiah James (1795-1851),

previously in Italy. Tradition has it that due to the superstition of the sailors his body was shipped back to Cork hidden in an upright piano in which it was subsequently placed in the family vault at Carrigrohane. The account of his funeral in the *Cork Examiner* of 12 January 1852, gives the clue as to the origin of this colourful tale: 'The usual coffin was enclosed in a large mahogany case, in which it had been brought over from Florence.' He is described as 'the friend of the poor and the father of the orphan, one who we rightly believe had never made a single enemy, but who

AUCTIONS.

AUCTION OF JAMAICA SUGAR.

JAMES, NICHS., and JEREMIAH MURPH
will Sell by Auction, on TUESDAY next, 7th May,
Hall's, One o'Clock,
100 *Hhds. JAMAICA SUGAR,*
which they are now landing *at* Ringmahon Castle, dire
April 30

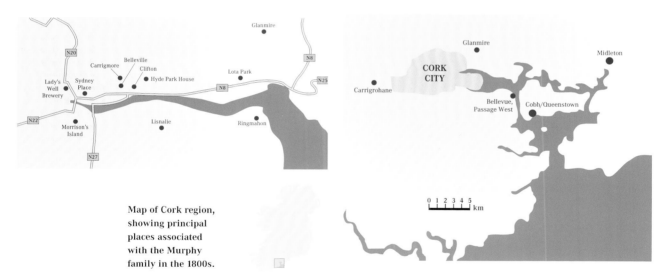

Map of Cork region, showing principal places associated with the Murphy family in the 1800s.

father of the brothers who founded Lady's Well Brewery. He married Catherine Bullen in 1818; they had fifteen children, nine daughters and six sons. They lived at Morrison's Island in the city until 1838 when they moved to Lota Park, near Glanmire, on the north side of the River Lee. Jeremiah James received a house at 8 Sydney Place as a gift and it was there his wife Catherine died in 1872. He had died twenty-one years

possessed many devoted friends even in the ranks of his strongest political opponents'. The article also recounts his many 'acts of unostentatious benevolence - of families secretly relieved, of ruin averted, of desolation prevented, of happiness conferred'.

Probably the most famous of the sons of James Murphy of Ringmahon was John (see highlight, pp. 15-16). He was educated in England

5

Murphy Family Tree
abridged

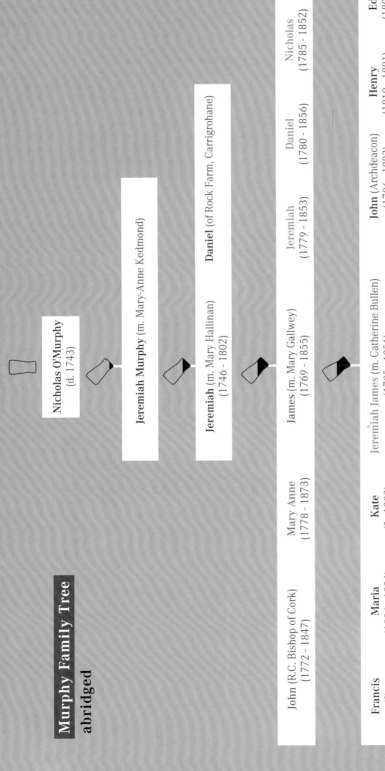

Nicholas O'Murphy
(d. 1743)

Jeremiah Murphy (m. Mary-Anne Kedmond)

Jeremiah (m. Mary Hallinan)
(1746 - 1802)

Daniel (of Rock Farm, Carrigrohane)

James (m. Mary Gallwey)
(1769 - 1855)

Mary Anne
(1778 - 1873)

John (R.C. Bishop of Cork)
(1772 - 1847)

Jeremiah
(1779 - 1853)

Daniel
(1780 - 1856)

Nicholas
(1785 - 1852)

Jeremiah James (m. Catherine Bullen)
(1795 - 1851)

John (Archdeacon)
(1796 - 1883)

Edward J.
(1801 - 1888)

Henry
(1810 - 1891)

Anna Maria
(1794 - 1869)

James
(1797 - 1875)

William
(? - 1799)

Kate
(? - 1883)

Maria
(1806 - 1834)

Francis
(?)

Nicholas
(1808 - 1834)

James Jeremiah (m. Ellen Gallwey)
(1825 - 1897)

Jerome
(1833 - 1899)

Francis
(1837 - 1919)

Susan
(1838 - 1838)

Emily
(1832 - 1832)

Frances Mary
(1840 - ?)

Emily
(1842 - 1908)

Ellen
(1837 - 1837)

Nicholas
(1834 - 1912)

William
(1828 - 1889)

Anne
(1821 - 1890)

John
(1830 - 1859)

Frances
(1823 - 1839)

Mary
(1820 - 1890)

Katherine
(1819 - 1878)

Albert St. John
(1859 - 1952)

James Fitzjames (m. Winifred Mary Murphy)
(1870 - 1946)

Jeremiah Francis
(1854 - 1887)

Charles Eustace
(1863 - 1951)

Arthur William
(1860 - 1876)

Harry Michael
(1857 - 1887)

Elizabeth
(1853 - 1853)

Edmund Burke
(1861 - 1879)

Victor Raymond
(? - 1913)

John Fitzjames (The Colonel)
(1909 - 1980)

Eileen
(1906 - 1977)

Cartoon celebrating the 1865 election campaign of Nicholas Dan Murphy, MP (centre right, with right arm outstretched). Bishop John Murphy, who died in 1847, is seated to the right. Other members of the extended Murphy family are gathered around them. The Murphys' involvement in distilling, brewing, shipping and trade is celebrated in the foreground and background.

Bust of James Murphy of Ringmahon (1769-1855) by John Hogan.

and led an adventurous life before being ordained a priest. He ministered in Liverpool and later Cork where he became Archdeacon and was responsible for the building of the church of SS Peter and Paul in the city.

James Murphy of Ringmahon, the father of these and ten other children, died on 10 November 1855. His obituary in the Cork Examiner describes him as

one of the first merchants of his native city . . . venerable in respect, courtly in manner, kind and tender to the distressed. [He] was an intense Catholic, devoted to his Church, proud of its sufferings as of its triumphs, the munificent contributor to every attempt to erect a chapel, to found a convent, to establish a school.

The only daughter of Jeremiah Murphy and Mary Hallinan was Mary Anne Murphy (1778-1873). She married a John Murphy in 1801 and they had two children, Michael and Jeremiah John, who was a QC. She lived at Lisnalie (probably Lisnalee) in Ballintemple, a suburb of Cork and is said to have 'devoted her widowhood to the gratuitous education of the poor girls of Blackrock parish.' The present National School in Ballintemple sprang from her original charitable work.

The fourth child of Jeremiah Murphy and Mary Hallinan was also called Jeremiah Murphy (1779-1853). He married Mary Stack and they lived at Hyde Park House in Montenotte. They had six children, the most well-known being Jeremiah Stack Murphy, who became the first Catholic MP in Cork in 1829, and Francis Stack Murphy who was MP for Cork, from 1837 until 1853.

Daniel Murphy (1780-1856) was the fifth child of Jeremiah Murphy and Mary Hallinan. He married Frances (Fanny) Donegan in 1804 and they lived at Belleville, also in the suburb of Montenotte. Daniel established the very successful tanning business, Daniel Murphy and Sons, which prospered in the Blackpool area of the

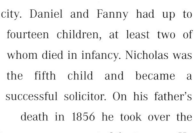

city. Daniel and Fanny had up to fourteen children, at least two of whom died in infancy. Nicholas was the fifth child and became a successful solicitor. On his father's death in 1856 he took over the management of the tannery. He was MP for Cork between 1865 and 1882 and lived at Lauriston, which is situated to the northeast of the city, near Glanmire.

Nicholas Murphy (1785-1852) was the youngest of the children of Jeremiah Murphy and Mary Hallinan. He married Susan Donegan in 1812 and they had fifteen children. They lived in Montenotte at Clifton, a substantial house, quite close to those of his brothers Jeremiah and Daniel. Nicholas was one of the co-founders of the distillery, James Murphy and Co., and his obituary states that 'as a merchant, Mr Murphy was remarkable for extraordinary ability . . . [and] unblemished integrity'. Like his brothers, he was renowned for his charity and he contributed greatly to the building of the Convent of Mercy, St Marie's of the Isle, in Cork. One of Nicholas's children, John Nicholas, also lived at Clifton and became Mayor of Cork in 1854 and High Sheriff of the city in 1857. He was also a devout Catholic and was the founding president of the St Vincent de Paul charity in Cork. He was responsible for the establishment of the Irish Sisters of Charity Children's Hospital and Convent on Wellington Road and donated the altar to the convent chapel of St Marie's of the Isle. John Nicholas was also a scholar whose books included *Ireland, Industrial, Political and Social, Terra Incognita,*

or the Convents of the United Kingdom and *The Chair of Peter,* 'a masterly vindication of the Papacy' for which he was made a Count of the Holy Roman Empire by the pope.

The ninth child of Nicholas, Frances Mary, became a nun in the Mercy Order in 1857 and in 1860 founded the Mercy Convent in Bantry, County Cork.

The youngest son of Nicholas of Clifton was also called Nicholas (1826-1909). He lived at Carrigmore in Montenotte and later at Norwood, near Cobh in County Cork. This Nicholas was an astute businessman and director of the distillery James Murphy and Co. In 1867 he steered the amalgamation of that firm and four city distilleries to form the Cork Distilleries Company. On his death in 1909 he left £251,488, an immense fortune for the time. Two of Nicholas's sons were also directors of the Cork Distilleries Co., Nicholas Philip of Myrtle Hill House, Tivoli and Norbert Nicholas of Lauriston, Glanmire. Their respective sons, Nicholas Stephen and Ronald Philip, also became directors of that firm and founders of Irish Distillers Ltd in 1966.

The fifth child of Nicholas of Carrigmore and Norwood was Muriel Frances. In 1917 she married Terence McSwiney, a prominent figure

Left: Bust of Daniel Murphy of Belleville (1780-1856) by John Hogan.

Muriel, daughter of Nicholas Murphy (1826-1909), pictured with her husband, Terence McSwiney, the Lord Mayor of Cork who died on hunger strike in 1920.

in the struggle for Irish independence. He became Lord Mayor of Cork and died in Brixton Prison in 1920, after over seventy days on hunger strike. Muriel became a communist activist and was very much the 'black sheep' of the family.

Jerome Murphy (second from right), brother of James J. and one of the brewery's founders, pictured with (from left) Hubert, Alfred, Carlo, Miss Daly (governess), Ernest Louis, Mary, Cyril and Cuthbert.

THE MURPHY COAT OF ARMS

The Murphy family coat of arms is now the brewery's company logo. It is a combination of two older coats, those of the O'Murphy sept of Muskerry and the O'Morchoe or Murphy sept of Wexford.

The colours, lions and cereal sheaves are all common features in heraldry and have no specific relevance to the Murphys. However, the fact that the dominant colours of red and white are those most associated with Cork (arising from the dominant rocks of sandstone and limestone), the link between the cereal sheaves and the brewing process, and the motto of 'Fortis et Hospitalis' ('strength and hospitality'), all combine to make the coat of arms a particularly appropriate logo for a Cork brewing family and company.

JAMES J. MURPHY (1825-1897)

Born on 10 November 1825, James Jeremiah Murphy was the eldest son of fifteen children born to Jeremiah James Murphy and Catherine Bullen. The family lived at Morrison's Island, near the city centre, later moving to Lota Park (now St Laurence Cheshire Home) and eventually to Sydney Place.

James J. married Ellen Gallwey in 1852 and lived at Bellevue, near Passage West, overlooking Cork Harbour. They had nine children, eight sons and one daughter. This daughter, called Elizabeth, was their first child and she died while still an infant. Tragedy visited the family again in later years. In 1876, their son, Arthur William, was drowned off the coast of Australia when he was swept from the deck of the *Allahabad* during the night of 24 July. He was only sixteen years old. Another son, Harry Michael, served in the Royal Navy and was drowned off Zanzibar in 1887 while serving on *HMS Reindeer*. A third son, Archie, died in July of that year in Sydney, Australia.

James J. served his time in the family business interests and was involved in the running of the Midleton distillery, founded by his grandfather and granduncles. He sold his share in the distilling company to fund his share of the set-up costs of Lady's Well Brewery in 1856. James J. was the senior partner in the new company, known as James J. Murphy & Co., the other partners being his brothers William, Jerome and Francis. A fifth brother, Nicholas, had a lesser role in the partnership and his interest was bought out in 1865.

James J. guided the brewery through the first forty years of its life and he saw its output grow to over 100,000 barrels per year before his death in 1897. His share of the profits of the brewery made him a wealthy man. In 1881, for example, James J. earned £11,250 as his share of that year's nett profits.

Banking was also an area of major interest to James J. He was a shareholder and director of the Munster Bank and in 1885 he endeared himself to many business people, ordinary depositors and shareholders when he led the venture that established the Munster and Leinster Bank. Earlier that year the Munster Bank had run into difficulties and was forced to cease trading. James J. gathered a number of other worthy businessmen around him and founded the new bank. The liabilities of the failed bank were taken over and eventually all creditors and depositors were repaid in full, with interest. This was a major achievement and a financial catastrophe was averted.

Such was the level of appreciation among the commercial and public bodies of Cork that, in 1890, a subscription was opened and 602 businessmen and gentlemen of the city

In Memoriam.

JEROME FRANCIS (Archie)
Died at Timoro, Sidney, New South Wales,
31st JULY, 1887.
In his 33rd Year.

HARRY M.
R.N., H.M.S. Reindeer, Drowned off Zanzibar
OCTOBER 25th, 1887,
In his 30th Year.

ARTHUR WILLIAM,
Drowned off Melbourne, from ship "Allahabad,"
JULY 24th, 1876,
In his 17th Year.

EDMUND BURKE,
Died at Passage, Co. Cork,
AUGUST 9th, 1879,
In his 17th Year.

Sons of J. J. Murphy, Bellevue, Passage

Memoriam card for four of the sons of James J. Murphy.

Left: James J. Murphy (1825-1897).

11

contributed to a presentation. At a function in the Imperial Hotel in Cork James J. was presented with two candelabra, bowls and other items, all of silver and appropriately engraved. He was also presented with an album of hand-illuminated addresses of gratitude and the names of all subscribers. The illuminated addresses came from the shareholders of the Munster and Leinster Bank, the Cork United Trades Association, the Cork Chamber of Commerce, the Cork Market Trustees, the Cork Butter Market, the Cork Harbour Commissioners and the City Council. At the presentation function it was stated:

The calamities which you averted by this action cannot be properly or adequately estimated; but we must record our conviction that if you, and those associated with you, had not assumed the task, the trade and commerce of the country would have been paralysed for many years, credit would have been destroyed, and misery and poverty would have fallen upon thousands of hapless victims.

All of the newspapers of the day, local and national, carried reports of the presentations and the full texts of the congratulatory speeches. The story was also reported in the brewing trade journals. *The Wine Merchant and Grocer's Review* of 24 August 1890 said that 'owing to the singularly retiring disposition of Mr Murphy, it was impossible for the outside public ever to realise the amount of gratitude which it owed him'. The account continued:

It is no exaggeration to say that he saved the nation from a dreadful calamity by the vast energy he displayed in liquidating the old

Munster Bank and establishing the new Munster and Leinster since the memorable crash in 1885. The labour to him seemed one of love, though there are few men of his wealth and position who would have undertaken it even at a princely compensation. Cork has every reason to be proud of such a man - a man who fulfils everything he promises, who never boasts of his achievements, who is a silent worker in this age of chatterboxes.

The Cork Vintners' Society made a separate presentation at another function. This consisted of a portrait in oils in which 'the likeness [of James J.] is faithful and the expression has been faithfully caught'. He was also presented with a framed illuminated address which included pictures of the brewery, of the family home at Bellevue and of a sinking ship, called *Munster*, being rescued by a lifeboat, called *Munster and Leinster*, symbolically representing the bank rescue. The portrait and framed address now hang in the brewery.

James J. was, as ever, modest in replying to the praises heaped upon him:

I did under the circumstances what I consider I was called on to do. I feel an honest pride in thinking we averted a dreadful calamity. I thank you gentlemen for the generous zeal you have exhibited to show me honour far beyond my

Silver presentation made to James J. Murphy in 1890 by the Munster and Leinster Bank shareholders, public bodies and businessmen of Cork.

Detail from an address to James J. Murphy from the Cork Vintners' Society, 1890. James J. is at the helm of the lifeboat, symbolising the new Munster and Leinster Bank, rescuing the crew of the stricken *Munster*, which represents the failed Munster Bank.

deserts. It will teach others that honest efforts to do good will be sure to win the respect and gratitude of all.

James J. became chairman of the new bank and the Murphy family was represented on the board until 1966, when the Munster and Leinster amalgamated with two other banks to become Allied Irish Banks.

Like his brothers, James J. was a keen sportsman and a member of the Royal Cork Yacht Club, the Glenbrook Rowing Club and the Cork Harbour Rowing Club. He was also a supporter of the Gaelic Athletic Association, then in its infancy, and donated a 'fifty-guinea cup' to the Cork County Board in 1891. The County Board had difficulty in deciding whether the trophy should be allocated to hurling or football. When James J. learned of this he donated another fifty guineas and 'stipulated that both cups shall be of local manufacture'. He was hailed by the GAA as one of its 'greatest friends' and the meeting of the Cork County Board of the association was adjourned as a mark of respect on the evening of his death.

James J. Murphy, like many of his forbears, was renowned for his generosity in contributing to charitable causes. His donations supported hospitals, orphanages and churches and subscriptions opened for the relief of distress invariably had a large contribution from James J. heading the list.

James J. Murphy died at his home on 26 October 1897 and was buried in the family vault at Carrigrohane. His obituaries and the accounts of his funeral in the newspapers of the day were fulsome in their praises: 'a giant in the commercial, he was a prince in the charitable world'. The brewery and bank he led stood 'as monuments to his extraordinary commercial ability and enterprise'. The requiem mass was held in the church of SS Peter and Paul and was attended by representatives of the professional, mercantile and public life of the city.

A ballad written in 1885 by Charles Jackson to honour James J. Murphy and celebrate his successes in banking and brewing. In the ballad he is referred to as 'Jerry James'.

13

The *Cork Examiner* reported:

As the cortege proceeded through the streets the people gathered in huge numbers to pay a last tribute of respect. Signs of mourning were everywhere displayed, many of the business establishments being shuttered. The weather was most inclement, and rain fell almost continuously from early morning. On arrival at the graveyard the burial service was read by Ven. Archdeacon Coughlan, and the coffin was then reverently placed in the family vault.

The widow of James J., Ellen, died twenty years later, on 26 June 1917. She was not buried with her husband, but in the graveyard of the Convent of Mercy in Passage West. A first cousin of James J., Sister Mary Austin (daughter of Henry Murphy, c. 1810-1891), had founded the convent and the Murphys had been among its benefactors.

One of the hand-illuminated addresses presented to James J. Murphy in 1890, showing the Munster and Leinster Bank premises in Cork and Dublin.

The Next Generations

Francis J. Murphy, brother of James J., succeeded him as chairman of the company following his death in 1897. Following the death of Francis, three of James J.'s sons in succession - Charles Eustace, Albert St John and finally Fitzjames - led the company. The sons were educated in Catholic public schools in England, and both Albert St John and Charles Eustace were prominent in hunting, cricket and rowing circles in Cork.

On the death of Fitzjames in 1946, his son John Fitzjames was recalled from service with the British Army where he held the rank of Lt Colonel. He served as a director until 1958 when he took over as chairman, a position he held until 1971. He became Honorary Life President of Murphys Brewery Ltd, the restructured successor to James J. Murphy & Co. Ltd, in 1974. The Colonel, as he was affectionately known, was the grandson of James J. and the last of his direct descendants to hold office at the brewery.

'The Black Eagle of the North'
ARCHDEACON JOHN MURPHY

John Murphy (1796-1883) was an uncle of James J. Murphy, founder of the brewery. He was a legendary Cork figure whose adventures included his being elected chief of a tribe of Canadian Indians who named him 'The Black Eagle of the North'.

At the age of eight or nine John was sent off to school in England, embarking at Cork's famous Coal Quay on one of his father's schooners, the *Mary and Betsy*. On leaving school he became a midshipman with the East India Company and sailed to China on the *Charles Grant*. In 1816, at the age of twenty, he went to work for the fur-trading Hudson Bay Company in North America. He was a daring frontiersman, 'always on the trail, carrying dispatches, fighting Indians, bringing provisions, making contact with trappers'. In 1818 he was put in charge of the company's fort at New Brunswick and remained there until 1822 when he sailed for England. There he became involved in commercial pursuits with his brothers and fell into heavy debt, which he eventually cleared when he inherited a large sum of money from his father.

Following his adventures in the commercial world, John apparently returned to Canada. While involved in trapping, he fell in with an Indian tribe with whom he 'wandered through the wilds' for a number of years. 'Crowned with feathers, dressed in skins, and with a painted face, the Indians loved him. He was elected their chief and was known as "The Black Eagle of the North".'

Accounts differ, but it seems that in the late 1830s John Murphy decided to become a Catholic priest and he sailed for Rome, via England, to begin his studies. He was ordained in 1843 at the age of forty-seven and went to work as a curate among the poor Irish immigrants in Liverpool. He was recalled to Cork in 1847 (by Bishop Delaney, his uncle John's successor) during the height of the Great Famine and was posted to Bandon. After a few months he was sent, apparently at his own request, to the Goleen/Schull area of west Cork where a local landowner and Protestant clergyman, William Fisher, had successfully won many converts to Protestantism during the famine. Fisher ran soup-kitchens and organised the converts in various 'relief work' schemes, including the building of a chapel known as Teampall na mBocht, or the Church of the Poor, in the parish of Kilmoe. In the eyes of the Catholic Church, Fisher's activities were a classic example of hated 'souperism', which used hunger as an instrument to win converts to Protestantism. Fr John Murphy arrived to counter this movement. He was a striking figure, riding a large black horse and spending 'lavishly of his own fortune' and probably that of his family. On Sunday mornings he stood on the walls outside Teampall na mBocht exhorting the converts to return to the Catholic faith. Having 'won back' a large number of converts, he was recalled to Cork with his mission accomplished.

Fr Murphy (the 'Famine priest') was appointed administrator of the Middle Parish in the city in 1848 and undertook fundraising for the building of the new church of SS Peter and Paul, designed by E. W. Pugin, which opened in 1866. He secured the lease of the old Cork Mansion House and in 1857 it became the Mercy Hospital, the first hospital in Cork to be placed in the charge of a religious order. The conversion cost £3,793, £300 of which was paid by Fr Murphy himself; James J. Murphy & Co. subscribed £100, as did James Murphy of Ringmahon and James Murphy & Co. distillery.

John Murphy was made Arch-deacon of Cork in 1874 and in the same year retired to private apartments at St Vincent's, Sunday's Well. He died there on 10 March 1883 and was interred in the Murphy family vault at Carrigrohane.

'La Petite Morfi'
MARIE LOUISA MURPHY

Marie Louisa Murphy (1737-1814) is famous as the mistress of King Louis XV of France and a favoured model of the court painter, Francois Boucher. According to brewery tradition she was the daughter of Daniel Murphy ('Dan the Cobbler'), an ancestor of the brewery founders, and the money she sent back from France provided the 'seed capital' for the Murphy family's business ventures.

Marie Louisa (also referred to as Marie Louise and as O'Murphy) was born in Rouen in 1737, the fifth daughter of Irish parents, Daniel Murphy and Margaret Hickey. Her father had been a soldier in the French army and subsequently became a shoemaker. Following his death the family moved to Paris and her mother worked as a second-hand clothes dealer near the Palais Royal. Her eldest sister became a model at the Academy of Painting and the young Marie Louisa followed in her footsteps,

sitting first for Boucher at the age of about thirteen. Louis XV is said to have become smitten by the young beauty and in March 1753 she became the first occupant of the Parc-aux-Cerfs, Versailles, a legendary house where Louis kept his mistresses. She gave birth to a child there in May 1754, but in the following year 'La petite Morfi', as Marie Louisa came to be known, was pushed out by Madame de Pompadour, the king's permanent mistress.

Marie Louisa married an elderly army officer in 1755, by whom she had a son. Her husband was killed two years later and she married a court official, who died in 1783. She was imprisoned as a 'suspect' during the 'Reign of Terror' following the French Revolution and after her release she married a revolutionary politician called Dumont, nearly thirty years her junior. They divorced in 1799 and Marie Louisa died in Paris on 11

December 1814, aged seventy-seven.

'La petite Morfi' became established in the public mind as 'the Girl in the Boucher', lying naked across a sofa, propped up on her elbows. She subsequently, and mistakenly, became the girl in all the Bouchers, including those which he painted before he had even met her. However, it is likely that the model featured in 'Ruhendes Mädchen' (1752), reproduced here, which hangs in the Alte Pinakothek in Munich, is indeed Marie Louisa Murphy.

What basis in fact is there for the brewery legend mentioned at the outset? Unfortunately for the romantics, there is very little. The historical evidence suggests that Marie Louisa Murphy had no connection whatsoever with the Cork Murphys. The confusion probably arose from the fact that both James J. Murphy's granduncle and Marie Louisa's father were called Daniel Murphy, they lived in the same era, and both had a connection with the leather trade.

Marie Louisa Murphy, as painted by Francois Boucher in c.1752, in a painting entitled 'Ruhendes Mädchen', which hangs in the Alte Pinakothek in Munich.

2

Brewing and Cork

BREWING

Origins

Brewing, in its simplest form, is the process of producing alcoholic drinks from starchy raw materials, such as barley, by steeping in water, boiling, usually with hops, and fermenting. It is not possible to state with any certainty when or where the process was first developed or invented. It is most likely that brewing developed in tandem with agriculture, beginning as early as 8,000 years ago. Around that time, in the fertile regions of the eastern Mediterranean, wild cereals were first 'tamed' and grown in an organised way by the first farmers. The relatively easy production of these cereals gave the people a staple food enjoyed as a raw whole grain or crushed and eaten as a simple porridge or bread. Archaeological evidence suggests that the potential of grains for producing alcoholic beverages was quickly recognised and exploited.

In the beginning, it is probable that barley was buried in pots to cause germination of the grains. This 'malt', mixed with water, would have fermented through the action of airborne yeasts to produce a very basic beer. Once established, the brewing process was refined and improved in a variety of ways. The fermentation, for example, could be induced by a measured addition of yeast, thus introducing a level of control into the process.

The flavour was improved through the addition of other ingredients. Herbs, bitter fruits and other materials were added to brews to give a bitterness to balance the sweetness of the malt. Bog myrtle, rosemary, camomile, yarrow and a range of other plants and fruits were used for this purpose. Hops, which today are the standard additive, were grown and used in the Middle East as early as 2,000 years ago.

Spread of Brewing

As agriculture developed and spread into Europe, so too did brewing. It took a firm hold in western and northern Europe in particular, where the growing of grapes for wine-making was not possible. Beer was an integral part of the diet of early agricultural societies because of its nutritional value. Also, alcoholic drinks have always been incorporated into a variety of religious and ritual practices and have formed a key part of hospitality customs. Thus, for thousands of years, brewing and beer drinking have been integral activities in a wide range of societies and cultures.

Ireland

Between 5,000 and 6,000 years ago agriculture became established in Ireland and it is probable that beer-making of some form was practised there from that time. The earliest Irish literature was first written in the seventh and eighth centuries AD by monastic scribes. It consists of tales and sagas, accounts of the lives of saints, ancient laws, etc., and contains many references to brewing and the drinking of beer.

Eighteenth-century engraving of a small scale brewery.

HOPS

Hops have been called 'the grapes of brewing'. Barley malt is essential to provide sugars for fermentation, but hops add bitterness, complex flavours and vital preservatives which keep the beer in better condition for longer. It is the dried cones of the hop, usually of the variety Humulus Lupulus, that are used. Prior to the introduction of hops into European brewing, brewers used to place a bag of mixed herbs and spices called 'gruit' in their ales before fermentation. Though hops were grown in Europe from as early as the eighth century, it was not until the thirteenth century that they began to challenge 'gruit' in Germany; from there, the use of hops spread and became the standard ingredient, along with malt, in brewing. Hops were used first in Britain in the fifteenth century.

Other plants were still used in British and Irish brewing in the early eighteenth century, but the success of highly hopped porter in the middle of that century saw the final triumph of the hop over other bittering agents. The original distinction between ale and beer was that the latter was brewed with hops and the former without. This distinction gradually disappeared and, following the development of porter, 'beer' and 'ale' were popularly used to to denote light coloured drinks as opposed to the darker porter and stout. In brewing, the term 'beer' covered all fermented drinks made from malted barley.

a. Lupulus fœmina, Houblon sauvage, Wilder Hopffen.
b. Lupulus Mas, Houblon, Hopffen.
c. Lupulus Mechiocanus.

20

Monk brewing, from
a medieval
manuscript.

Medieval Monastic Brewers

In medieval Europe, the large monasteries were important centres of agriculture, scholarship and science. They housed large numbers and in many instances were virtually self-sufficient. The monks farmed to feed their communities and brewed beer as a normal and essential means of providing nourishment and refreshment. Later, beer was also sold to support the monastic communities. These medieval monasteries refined brewing methods and improved techniques, just as those in vine-growing regions contributed to improvements in wine-making.

Brewing and Beer-drinking in Medieval Ireland

From about the twelfth century, towns began to develop in Britain and Ireland, particularly at ports and on navigable rivers. Simple commercial brewing operations were established in these growing towns, and the brewing and selling of beer was carried on in the same premises. The wealthy brewed for their own needs in 'home' brewhouses. Brewing at that time was frequently the preserve of women, the so-called 'ale-wives'.

The popularity of beer in medieval times was due not only to its intoxicating qualities. Beverages such as coffee, tea and cocoa were not yet known in Europe, while water supplies, particularly in the towns and cities, were highly unreliable in terms of hygiene. The boiling of water during the brewing process and the anti-bacterial properties of alcohol produced a relatively sterile and safe drink.

Alehouses

Alehouses or taverns grew in number in the sixteenth century. The owners brewed their own drink and most did their own malting. Alehouses and taverns proliferated in Cork and Dublin during the seventeenth century, and in 1635 they were licensed for the first time. The Cromwellians, who arrived in Ireland in 1649, made some efforts to limit the number of alehouses, and in 1653 the sale of beer was banned altogether for a time in Cork. Drinking establishments continued to thrive, however, and in 1674 the poet Dáibhí Ó Bruadair wrote that the town of Cork was notable for its 'gaily lighted ale shops' with their 'many quarts and pints and many draughts of beer . . . Heart's desire for tipplers'.

The Advent of Porter

In the alehouses and taverns of eighteenth-century England, mixtures of beers became

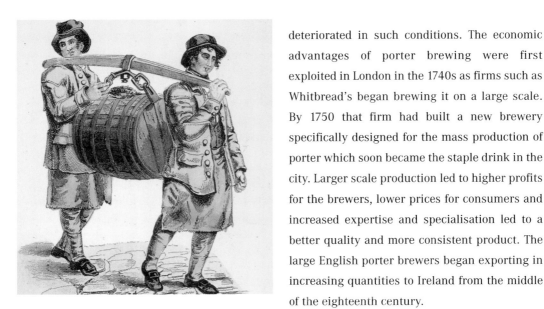

popular, and one mixture (probably consisting of pale ale, new brown ale and stale brown ale) was known as 'three threads'. A brewer called Ralph Harwood, in Shoreditch in East London, is said to have produced in 1772 a single, dark coloured beer which incorporated the characteristics of 'three threads'. Because it was drawn from a single butt or cask, as opposed to three separate ones, the new drink was initially known as 'Entire Butt' or simply 'Entire'. Its popularity with manual labourers, and especially the market porters in the vicinity, led to it being renamed 'porter's ale' or simply 'porter'.

The initial advantage of porter arose from the fact that it could be made from relatively cheap, coarse barley and less refined hops which suited London's soft water. Its more important advantages took time to emerge and were to transform the brewing industry in Britain and Ireland. Its most important asset was that it could be made in bulk, maturing best in large containers and actually improved if left to mature for a year or so. This was not the case with the lighter, clearer beers of the time which

deteriorated in such conditions. The economic advantages of porter brewing were first exploited in London in the 1740s as firms such as Whitbread's began brewing it on a large scale. By 1750 that firm had built a new brewery specifically designed for the mass production of porter which soon became the staple drink in the city. Larger scale production led to higher profits for the brewers, lower prices for consumers and increased expertise and specialisation led to a better quality and more consistent product. The large English porter brewers began exporting in increasing quantities to Ireland from the middle of the eighteenth century.

The dark colour of the original porter was achieved by the employment of a considerable proportion of highly dried 'brown malt' in the mixture of malts used in brewing. In 1817 a new development was patented by Daniel Wheeler. This involved replacing the brown malt by a much smaller proportion of a more highly coloured malt made by drying at a much higher temperature, in other words, roasting. This 'patent malt' marked the beginning of the history of porter (and stout) as it is known today, and ended the period during which the term 'porter' was probably applied to any brown beer to distinguish it from pale ale.

Brewing in Ireland in the Eighteenth Century

The eighteenth century saw the increasing commercialisation of brewing in Europe and Britain, facilitated in the latter by the development of porter. This process was slower in Ireland where the industry for most of the century continued to be dominated by retail brewers, i.e. publicans who brewed on their

The 'masses' of Cork had a reputation for riotous behaviour, and food riots, looting and clashes with the police in connection with strikes and elections were a frequent occurrence throughout the century. There was a distinct lack of social radicalism, however, and the powerful and wealthy did not have their position threatened. There were a number of reasons for this. The dominance of small–scale manufacturing and the fact that only the conservative skilled trades were organised militated against large-scale mobilisation of the working class on social and economic issues. Popular politics were dominated by nationalism in its various manifestations, and the 'masses' were encouraged to see the movements such as those for Repeal of the Union and Home Rule as a panacea for their ills. This suited the propertied class whose members led these movements and whose position was further bolstered by the support of the Catholic clergy and the press.

Politics and Religion

In the last four decades of the nineteenth century the population of the city was approximately 84 per cent Catholic, 13 per cent Protestant, and 3 per cent Dissenter or 'other'. Political and religious divisions overlapped, with Catholics usually being identified as liberal and nationalist and Protestants as conservative and unionist. Merchants (Catholic and Protestant) dominated municipal politics for most of the century and the commercial, manufacturing and professional classes monopolised parliamentary representation also. One of the extended Murphy family, Nicholas Dan (see Chapter 1) held one of the city's two seats in the parliament at Westminster in four consecutive elections up to 1880, when he was replaced by Charles Stewart Parnell. He was most prominent in opposing the restrictions on Sunday opening times for public houses in the 1870s, both because of his family ties to the drink industry (brewing and distilling) and the strength of the vintners' lobby in the city.

Sport and Recreation

During the last forty years of the century the number of pubs in Cork city averaged 550 for a population of around 78,000. This amounted to one pub for every 1,420 people or 660 males, though women and children also visited pubs, which were the primary recreational venues for the majority of the population. During deliberations on the introduction of Sunday closing of pubs in 1876 the police in Cork were enlisted to count the numbers who used them. On two selected Sundays in that year it was estimated that 37 per cent of the total population of the city entered a pub. Publicans served other functions besides supplying drink. They acted as moneylenders and as paymasters to unskilled labourers, especially dockers. In the early part of the century 'sports' such as bare fisted boxing and cockfighting were common. Other sports, which are still popular today, included road bowling and the keeping of harriers, while in the latter part of the century the GAA provided an important sporting and social outlet for the 'ordinary people'.

The lives of the wealthy citizens of Cork, like the Murphys, were in stark contrast to those of the majority of the population. They lived in splendid houses on the outskirts of the city, were educated and holidayed abroad, engaged in sports like cricket and rowing, and entertained lavishly, with three or four seven-course dinners per week not unusual.

3

James J. Murphy & Co.: The Early Years 1856-1883

By the middle of the nineteenth century the Murphy family had already established its name as a significant force in the drinks industry. The Midleton distillery of James Murphy & Co. had been founded in 1825 and had grown spectacularly. By the 1850s it was quite profitable and had become the principal distillery in the Cork area, employing over 180 people. The brewing industry was then showing potential for growth and James J. Murphy & Co. was established in 1856 to operate Lady's Well Brewery. The Murphy name was set to preside over another success. James J. Murphy and his brothers William, Jerome, Francis and Nicholas were the partners in the new brewing venture and they 'applied themselves with energy and enterprise' to emulate their grandfather and granduncles who had set up the successful Midleton distillery.

Brewery Construction

James J. and his brothers purchased the buildings of the Cork Foundling Hospital in 1854 and over the following two years some of those buildings were adapted and others newly built and 'the parties erected there divers works and machinery for brewing and the same premises are now called the Lady's Well Brewery'. The construction of the new brewery was supervised by Gresham Wiles, a brewer who had been brought from London by the Murphys.

The construction work caused some controversy as the Foundling Hospital chapel had to be demolished to make way for the brewery. The chapel had a much admired stained-glass window and interior and the Rev. W. C. Neligan, rector of St Mary's, made great, but unsuccessful, efforts to save the building.

The hospital buildings had been purchased for £1,300 and by September 1857 almost £25,000 had been spent on bringing the brewery to a satisfactory operating level.

A ledger from the period summarises the costs as follows:

Purchase	£1,300		
Stone and mortar	£844		
Timber	£1,400		
Gas fittings	£254		
Boilers, engines, mash tun pipes etc.	£4,278		
Vats and tanks	£2,817		
Smiths' work	£400		
Labour, masons, carpenters etc. and sundry materials	£5,233	3s	5d
Gerald Mahony, constrcts.	£1,114		
John Penny for sundries	£240		
Drays, floats and trucks	£197	12s	
7 horses	£264	5s	6d
Harness	£57	2s	6d
2,120 sacks	£163	3s	4d
Cards, labels and frames	£356	7s	10d
7,929 casks	£4,776	13s	
Glen Distillery for materials	£250		
John Hart, cooler, in progress	£300		

Expenditure on buildings continued in the following years. In addition to general maintenance it was necessary to increase brewing capacity in line with growing demand. In 1858 £1,951 was spent on buildings, in 1859 £4,479 and £3,904 in 1860.

£1 = 20s
1s = 12d

Detail from a painting of Lady's Well Brewery, c.1870.

The surviving façade and gateway of the Cork Foundling Hospital on Leitrim Street.

THE CORK FOUNDLING HOSPITAL

In 1854 the Murphy brothers purchased the buildings of the Cork Foundling Hospital for £1,300 and set about adapting them for use as a brewery.

The hospital had been opened in 1747 to care for the abandoned and unwanted children of the city. It was financed by a tax of 1s per ton of coal and culm imported into Cork and by weigh-house fines and penalties on car-drivers. A board of governors over-saw the running of the institution and all children in their care were to be instructed in the Protestant religion.

Infants were accepted by the hospital only at Eastertime; those abandoned at other times of the year were the responsibility of parish church wardens. Many children were brought from country districts to be abandoned in the city in the hope that they might eventually be taken into the hospital. In the early 1800s a commentator complained that Cork had become 'the gathering place for all the bastards of the South of Ireland'.

Once accepted, infants were branded under the arm. They were then put out to wet-nurses to be cared for until they were six or seven years old. Wet-nurses were paid and the branding was to prevent the sub-stitution of another child should that being cared for die. Many of the infants and young children in the care of the hospital did die. Between 1820 and 1833, for example, 3,247 children were received, of whom 2,018 died.

When the children returned to the hospital from their wet-nurses, they were given rudimentary education, principally in the tenets of the Protestant faith. They were kept until old enough to be apprenticed to Protestant masters. At any one time between 200 and 500 children were being kept in the hospital while a similar or greater number was in the care of wet-nurses.

Even by the standards of the time the Foundling Hospital was not a pleasant place for children. It was said that 'there is too little attention to cleanliness' and that the children looked 'dejected and unhappy'. In 1838 the Poor Relief Act provided for the closure of the hospital. The number of inmates was gradually reduced until 1854, when only twenty-four remained. These were transferred to the Cork Workhouse.

The Poor Law Guardians wanted the hospital buildings to become an emigration depot and also offered them to the military as a barracks, but without success. Eventually the former Cork Foundling Hospital was offered for sale to the public and purchased by James J. Murphy and his brothers.

Parts of the hospital buildings and the original gateway survive, fronting on to Leitrim Street.

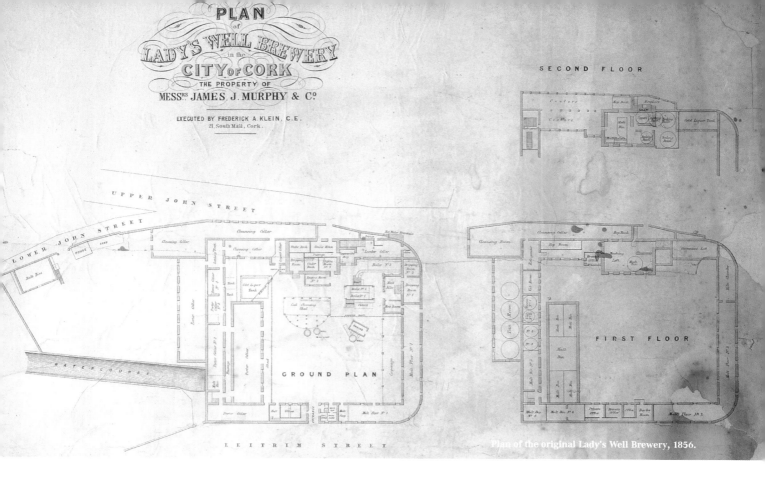

PLAN
of
LADY'S WELL BREWERY
in the
CITY of CORK
THE PROPERTY OF
MESS.RS JAMES J. MURPHY & C.O

EXECUTED BY FREDERICK A KLEIN, C.E.
21 South Mall, Cork.

SECOND FLOOR

FIRST FLOOR

GROUND PLAN

Plan of the original Lady's Well Brewery, 1856.

OUR LADY'S WELL

Our Lady's Well, from which the brewery takes its name. It is located on the high ground above Leitrim Street.

Our Lady's Well, which gives its name to the brewery, is a 'holy well' situated on a hill across from the brewery on Leitrim Street, Cork. It is reputed to have been a place of devotion for Catholics since the Penal Days of the eighteenth century. During that century it was also used as a water source by the inhabitants of the area. A shrine was established there and pilgrimages took place in the month of May, including a major one from Maynooth in 1748.

The grotto gradually fell into disrepair and the statue of the Virgin Mary which stood there was destroyed by vandals. In 1979 employees at Lady's Well Brewery began collecting funds for its restoration and in 1983 a concelebrated mass was held at the refurbished site.

James J. Murphy

William Murphy

Jerome Murphy

Francis Murphy

The Partnership

James J. Murphy and his brother William were the principal partners, having a one-third share each. The other three brothers each had a one-ninth share. James J. and William had contributed the largest proportion of the building costs. They financed this by selling their shares in the Midleton distillery, James Murphy & Co., for £10,000 each and through an inheritance of £2,500 each from their grandfather, James Murphy of Ringmahon, who had died in 1855. The profits or losses of the new firm were to be shared by the partners in proportion to their respective holdings.

In December 1865 the nature of the partnership changed when Nicholas gave up his one-ninth share in return for an annual payment of £400. In 1872 the relative shareholdings changed again. From that year James J. and William held a three-eighths interest each and Jerome and Francis one-eighth each.

Brewing Begins

Brewing in the 1850s, and indeed for some time afterwards, was not a very exact science. While the quality of the principal ingredients of water, malted barley and hops was very important, the success of the final product depended greatly on the skills and experience of the brewer. Prior to the development of sensitive scientific controls, the observations of the brewer and his ability to control the various stages of the brewing process were crucial to the production of quality beers.

When Lady's Well Brewery went into production in 1856, Edward Lane held the position of head brewer. He was paid an annual salary of £600 and, in addition, received £400 per year from nett profits. This was a huge income at a time when an unskilled worker at the brewery earned 10s for a week's work and a skilled carpenter or cooper earned between £1 and £1 5s per week. Lane appears to have been successful in producing 'a liquor at once combining strength of body with excellence of flavour'.

Ledger entry for the year ending 31 October 1858, summarising the brewery's income (right) and expenditure (left). Porter was sold at 28s 5d per barrel, ale at 37s 6d per barrel.

Lady's Well Ale and Murphy's Porter

James J. Murphy & Co. initially brewed porter and ale. The ale was called Lady's Well Ale and a newspaper account of the new brewery in 1857 tells us:

To the judicious management of the hopping is mainly due the mild and pleasant flavour of the 'Lady's Well Ale' manufactured at Messrs Murphy's brewery and which bids fair to acquire an extended popularity.

In 1858 2,020 barrels of ale were sold. The following year the figure was 900 barrels and in 1860 it rose a little to 950 barrels. Output fell again in 1861 and ale was not brewed after that date. Murphy's Porter was far more successful and was the brewery's sole product from 1862 until 1889 when stout was introduced. Figures begin for 1858 when sales were 20,705 barrels. This had risen to 42,990 by 1861.

The head brewer, Edward Lane, left the brewery in 1862. The reason for his departure is not known. Production was interrupted until a new brewer, Edward Herring, was appointed in May of that year. The agreement he signed with James J. Murphy & Co. states:

His salary to be Six Hundred pounds a year, and in the event of his making ale and stout in addition to draft porter, entirely to their [the partners'] satisfaction and approval, they will increase such salary by £400 a year.

This agreement indicates that it was more difficult to brew ale and stout than porter, and that a brewer with the requisite skill could command a substantial income. Edward Herring's career with the brewery was short-lived. He left after only three months, in August 1862.

Output fell as a result of these changes and averaged around 36,000 barrels for 1862 and 1863. These teething problems were apparently overcome and output recovered in subsequent years.

THE BREWING PROCESS AND ITS INGREDIENTS

Malting

Malted barley, hops and water are the principal ingredients of porter. County Cork is especially suited to the growing of barley and James J. Murphy & Co. bought most of its requirements locally. The company had a malt house in Riverstown, east of Cork city, and malted barley there. A lesser amount of barley was malted at the brewery and if more was needed it was bought in.

The amount of malt used by the brewery rose in line with output from 13,034 barrels in 1858 to 43,371 barrels in 1883. The cost of barley and malt varied from year to year, depending on the quality of the crop and demand. Costs to the brewery over the 1858 to 1883 period ranged from as low as 23s per barrel in 1881, to a high of 41s 1d in 1867.

In the malt house the barley was first steeped in water under controlled temperatures and then drained and piled in heaps or 'couches'. Once germination began the barley was spread more thinly by raking and was frequently turned. Careful temperature control was again essential at this stage. Having germinated, the grains were dried in kilns, and this drying stopped further germination. Some malt was roasted to a dark colour and was used in the brewing with pale malt and roasted unmalted barley to give the porter its characteristic dark

£1 = 20s
1s = 12d

colour and taste. In 1859 the brewery lost 1,758 barrels of malt when fire broke out at one of its malt houses. The loss was valued at £2,975.

Mashing

For brewing, the malt was first ground to produce 'grist' and was then mixed with hot water. This stage was called 'mashing' and occurred in vessels called 'mash tuns'. When mashing was complete the resulting solution, called 'wort', was separated from the spent grains, drawn off and fed to the 'copper', a large domed copper vessel. The spent grains from the mashing process were sold to farmers as animal feed.

Hopping

In the copper the hops were added to the wort. As Ireland's climate does not suit the cultivation of hops these were imported, usually from the south-east of England. As with malt, the quantities used each year varied in proportion to the amount of porter brewed. Hops were bought by the hundredweight (cwt) (1cwt = 50kgs approx.). In 1860 850 cwt of hops were used and this rose to over 2,000 cwt by the early 1880s. Prices varied greatly, depending on the hop harvest, demand and freight charges. In 1860, for example, hops cost the brewery £5 per cwt, while the following year the cost more than

THE BREWING PROCESS

Brewing is an ancient process using the most basic ingredients - barley, hops and water. While science and technology have made important contributions, the stages of production remain relatively unchanged.

STAGE 1

Malts and roasted barley are crushed to form grist. This is then mixed with hot water in a large vat called a mash tun. (Roasted barley is used only in the brewing of stout.)

STAGE 2

This mixture is stirred and the starch in the barley is converted to sugar.

STAGE 3

The spent grains are separated and the liquid called liquor or sweet wort, is transferred to a boiling vessel called a copper.

STAGE 4

The wort is boiled and hops are added at this stage to balance the brew's distinctive taste and aroma. The hop residues are separated from the brew in a whirlpool.

STAGE 5

The hopped wort is cooled and pumped to the fermentation tanks. Here yeast is added and the process of fermentation begins. This converts the sugar to alcohol and carbon dioxide.

STAGE 6

After fermentation the beer (stout, lager or ale) is allowed to mature and mellow.

STAGE 7

Once mature, any yeast residues are removed, the beer is filtered and the carbon dioxide and nitrogen levels are adjusted. The final product is then racked, filled into kegs, bottled or canned.

doubled to an exceptional £11 4s 6d. Such a high price was very unusual, however, and in other years the prices were more reasonable, ranging between £4 10s and about £6.

Hops gave the porter 'an agreeable bitterness' and flavour and also aided the preservation of the brew. Timing and temperature control were of critical importance at this stage of the brewing process also as the brewer wanted sufficient heat to 'separate the aromatic portion of the plant without extracting the rank and injurious elements'.

Cooling

After hopping, the spent hops were separated and the wort was passed for cooling where refrigeration was achieved by running cold water through the numerous pipes which ran through the wort cooler. In advance of refrigeration using ammonia, ice was used to cool the water. This was stored in an ice house. An entry in a brewery account book of April 1862 notes that £5 14s was paid to William Daly for carting 114 loads of ice from a ship at George's Quay to the brewery's ice house.

Fermentation and Cleansing

The cooled wort passed to the fermentation tuns which had capacities of 200 and 500 barrels. The

The coal boat *Ellen Sutton* unloading at Morrison's Island.

yeast was added at this stage and two days' fermentation followed. The remnants of the yeast were then separated and the porter was drawn off and cleansed in the cleansing rounds. Here all impurities were removed before the porter was eventually brought to the vats, huge wooden vessels capable of holding over 500 barrels each.

The vats held the porter until it was 'racked' or filled into barrels in the racking cellar.

Sugar

Sugar was used in the manufacture of porter and was added at the hopping stage, when the wort was in the coppers. It was added to provide more fermentable material for the production of alcohol at the fermentation stage. The brewery records show that 43 cwt of sugar were used in 1858. Sugar is not mentioned again in the accounts until 1867, when 6,254 cwt were used. Quantities used rose to a maximum of about 15,000 cwt in the early 1880s.

The price was relatively static, at about £1 10s per cwt, until 1880, when it began to drop dramatically. This was due to a change in how brewing was taxed. Up to 1880 the malt and sugar used in brewing were taxed but after that date the tax or duty was levied on the beer produced. In 1889, the last year for which the relevant figures are available, the price paid by the brewery was 13s 4d per cwt.

Coal

Coal fired the boilers that produced the steam to heat the brews and drive the rollers and elevators and all the other machinery in the brewery. Coal was the principal fuel though gas was used for lighting. In the first years of its operation the brewery imported some of its coal directly, generally from Wales. From about 1867, however, it dealt principally with the coal-importing firm of Abraham Sutton of the South Mall in Cork.

The ledgers of the 1850s and 1860s give quite an amount of detail on the purchase and importing of coal. Cargos usually weighed about 200 tons and quantities like this were bought many times during the year. Once landed at the quays in Cork, the coal had to be carted to the brewery, where it was stored. A stockpile was always kept in the event of a restriction on supply.

Through the 1860s and 1870s the price of coal was relatively static, varying between 16s and 17s per ton. The years 1872 and 1873 were exceptional, however, in that coal averaged £1 5s 2d and £1 6s 6d per ton respectively, more than 50 per cent above the usual price.

The Newport Coal Co. in Wales supplied most of the coal used at the brewery, though there were some dealings with the South Wales Coal Co. and with some other suppliers also. The brewery accounts for the period record the names of the ships that carried the cargos to Cork: *Moonbeam*, *Herbert*, *Princess Royal*, *Rebecca*, *Girl I Love*, *Eliza*, *Petrel* and many more. Freight charges varied according to cargo, ranging from 5s 6d to more than 7s per ton. A ledger entry for April/May 1864 details one cargo as follows:

15 April 198 tons (weighed in as 198 tons, paid as 192) @ 10s per ton to Newport Coal Co. ex Moonbeam , £96.
13 May Freight on 198 tons @ 5s 6d + half dues 3s 9d, less £7, £47 12s 9d.
14 May Wm Daly for landing, carting 198 tons @ 1s per ton £9 18s.

This cargo of coal, bought at 10s per ton in Wales, cost 15s 6d delivered to the brewery. William Daly did all of the carting until 1867, when Daniel Murphy took over. Details of ships, tonnages and breakdowns of costs are not given after 1868. From then, only details of total tonnage of coal bought, with costs, is given.

Water

A plentiful supply of water was, and still is, fundamental to successful brewing. Though called Lady's Well Brewery, water was not taken from Our Lady's Well, a holy well situated on the high ground opposite the brewery on Leitrim Street. Wells were drilled within the brewery itself to provide water. A newspaper account of the opening of the brewery remarks:

They [Messrs Murphy] possess, however, one great advantage in having an inexhaustible supply of the purest well water, suitable for manufacturing the finest bitter and sweet ales.

At that time the water was pumped from a depth of sixty feet in the northern or upper courtyard. A tank, capable of holding 3,000 barrels was built with pipes feeding the supply to where it was needed. From 1859 supplies were taken from the municipal system for brewing purposes while the requirements for cooling, washing, etc. came from the brewery's own wells. Immense quantities of water were used at the brewery. It has been estimated that for every barrel of beer brewed, about twenty-five barrels of water were required.

Casks

The porter was filled into wooden barrels in the racking cellar. These barrels or casks came in four sizes: hogsheads, barrels, half-barrels, and kils. The hogshead had the largest capacity, fifty-two gallons, and was principally supplied to wholesalers for bottling. (The brewery did not directly bottle its own products until 1921). The barrel held thirty-two gallons and the half-barrel or kilderkin (shortened to kil), sixteen. The half-barrel was the most popular size as it was relatively easily handled by the rackers, draymen and publicans. The small eight-gallon firkin was less common.

The racking cellar (sometimes called a hall or shed) was one of the busiest and active parts of the brewery. Barrels were continually rolled to and from the racking vessels. The porter was fed from the racking vessel by tube to the bung-hole of the barrel. Thousands of barrels were necessary for the efficient working of the brewery. At any one time barrels were in use or storage in public houses, in transit, being repaired at the cooperage or being cleaned and filled at the brewery. While filled barrels were despatched relatively promptly, the empties were not always so quickly returned. Many disappeared and replacing such barrels to cope with increasing demand was a constant and significant expense. It was not until 1912 that a cask numbering system was introduced in an attempt to remedy the problem of straying barrels.

The coopers repaired and made casks or barrels in the brewery cooperage. This was initially situated in the northern or upper courtyard of the brewery but a newer and larger cooperage was later built opposite the brewery on Leitrim Street. Coopers were skilled craftsmen and enjoyed high rates of pay and privileges compared to the labourers at the brewery. Casks were in constant need of repair. On return to the brewery empties were examined

Coopers at work in the Lady's Well cooperage.

prior to cleaning and any in need of repair were transferred to the cooperage. (See highlight, p.106).

In the cask-washing shed the insides of the barrels were first cleansed with pebbles and hot water. They were then steamed before being cooled. As the brewery grew and became prosperous, the cleansing machinery was updated and renewed to the highest possible standards.

The accounts of the brewery show a not insignificant spending on materials for the making and repair of casks. In 1872 this amounted to £1,249 5s 8d and in 1874 £1,334 4s 9d. In addition, casks were occasionally bought from outside the brewery.

Stables, Horses and Drays

For the first sixty years or so of its life, the horse, in conjunction with the train, met the transport needs of the brewery. Indeed, it was to be over a century before the horse eventually gave way fully to mechanised transport in the 1960s. The barrels of porter were despatched from the upper yard in drays. These were two-wheeled carts drawn by one horse. These drays were quite low-slung to ease loading and unloading of barrels. The higher cart was known as a float. Later,

Murphy drays outside Lady's Well Brewery, from a painting *c.*1870.

bigger four-wheeled drays were used.

City deliveries were made directly from the brewery and orders for more distant destinations were brought to the different city railway stations for onward carriage.

The brewery stables were located on Leitrim Street, on the opposite side to the brewery. These housed seven horses at first, but the number had grown to nineteen by 1868. The maintenance of stables, drays and horses was a significant expense.

The first seven horses bought by the brewery cost £274 5s 6d, an average of nearly £40 each. Some detail survives on subsequent purchases of horses, but only for the period 1863 to 1872. There was great variation in prices. While some horses were bought for as little as £12 or £13, others cost up to £20 and more. On 16 July 1864, for example, £26 5s 6d was paid for a grey horse at Cahirmee, County Cork, the venue of an ancient horse fair. The names of some of the brewery horses of the 1860s and early 1870s are given in one of the old account books: Jasper, Dominic, Reynard, Sam, Captain, Actor, Noble, Major, Simon, Blackbird, Patrick, Dandy, Morgan, Rufus, Hair Oil and Champion.

There was, of course, a certain turnover in horses and on occasion a horse was exchanged or 'traded-in' as part of the purchase of a new animal. Others were sold at a price that suggests they were past their useful life. A brown mare was sold for £1 in January 1863 and another horse, Bessie, was sold in June 1865 for £1 19s. A new set of horse-harness cost about £8 at that time and harness repair was part of the occasional work done for the brewery by outside workers. A man called O'Keefe was paid £1 1s in October 1863 for one week's work repairing harnesses. From 1865 to 1869, at least, B. Foley did all the brewery harness work and was paid between £26 and £39 in each of those years for his work.

Feed for the horses was a major expense in the stables. The principal feeds were oats and hay, but Indian corn and carrots were also bought. The brewery owned or had the use of a number of hayfields at Riverstown, where one of the brewery malt houses was also located. Hay for the stables was cut there. Some of that work is detailed in the accounts for the early 1860s. In August 1862 £12 8s 2d was paid for 'men and women's time making hayrick at Riverstown'. William Daly was paid £2 7s 1d for the use of his horses and carts to draw the hay. Hay was also bought, usually at £2 to £2 10s per ton. Oats cost between 6s and 8s per cwt and in the year 1863 about 1,400 cwt of oats were bought at a total cost of £404 15s 10d.

Farriers were employed when necessary and Edward Ashe, William Sullivan and another man called Fleming are recorded as having shoed brewery horses during the 1860s.

The purchase and maintenance of the drays was another of the brewery's transport and carriage costs. In August 1864 R. Walsh was paid £3 12s 6d for a porter dray. In September 1866 M. O'Neill was paid £6 for making a dray. In April 1873 Timothy Herlihy received £24 for two drays. Prices varied, depending, presumably, on the size and state of the drays.

Constant maintenance was also necessary. The brewery had a wheelwrights' shop where repairs were carried out. The accounts for this early period show frequent purchases of wheel spokes: fifteen-and-a-half dozen bought in June 1870 for £2 6s 6d; twenty dozen bought in September 1871 for £4. Stocks, shafts and quantities of timber (ash) were also bought for the maintenance and repair of drays. Replacing the metal wheel-bands was also a frequent repair.

Other items purchased at this time for the stables included curry-combs, brushes, rugs, suits of oilskin for draymen, horse covers, cart covers and men's boots. The cost of running the stables, exclusive of wages, averaged about £500 per year in the early 1860s. By 1883 this had risen to £1,589.

The stables generated a little income for the brewery also. The manure from the stalls was sold. In 1863, for example, John McDonnell of Waterfall paid £12 10s for the manure of fifteen horses at 5d each per week from October 1862 to July 1863. The manure was sold on that basis every year.

Wages

Precise records of the wages paid to the brewery's employees do not survive for this period. However, occasional notes in the extant ledgers give some indication as to the rates of pay. In 1863 a carpenter was paid £1 for five days work. In 1863 James Lynch, a mason, was paid £1 5s for a week's work and 10s was paid to a man for assisting him. In the same year T. Daly, a cooper, earned £52 for one year's work. In 1866 a smith and his helper were paid £1 16s for their week at the brewery. Men, whose duties are unspecified, were paid 10s each per week.

These various figures suggest that craftsmen or tradesmen were paid between £1 and £1 6s per week, while unskilled workers received 10s. These rates were for a six-day week and paid holidays were not a feature of employment conditions at the time. It was not until the following century that wages saw any significant rise.

It is interesting to contrast these rates with the income of Edward Lane, the company's brewer in the early 1860s. He earned £1,000 per year or almost £20 per week. From 1869 Francis Murphy and his brother Jerome were each paid salaries of £400 per year as brewers. That was in addition to their share of the profits which they received as partners in the firm.

Seasonal factors affected the weekly wage bill at the brewery. More men were employed in the autumn months of August and September, when porter consumption was highest. The months of April and May tended to have the lowest wage costs.

It is not possible to establish how many men were employed at the brewery in the 1856 to 1883 period. In the 1860s the annual wage bill rose from £3,688 in 1862 to £4,520 in 1867, or from an average of about £71 per week to £87 per week. This would suggest that the average number employed was probably over one hundred by 1867, allowing for a much greater proportion of unskilled employees than craftsmen.

By 1872 the yearly wage bill had increased to

£8,602 or about £165 per week. This would indicate that up to two hundred were employed. The annual wage bill dropped every year after that to £6,000 in 1880 (for eleven months) or £125 per week. By 1883, when James J. Murphy & Co. became a joint stock company, these payments had risen again to £7,728 per annum or £148 per week.

In this period, the brewing industry, like most others, was very labour intensive and the day-to-day life of Lady's Well Brewery must, on occasion, have resembled the human equivalent of an ant colony. All raw materials were delivered by horse-drawn carts and unloaded by hand: coal and hops from the city's quays, barley from the countryside, malt from the Riverstown malt house. Straw and hay were delivered to the stables on a regular basis while manure was carted away by market gardeners. The brewery's drays were loaded and left through the old Foundling Hospital gate to deliver to the city's public houses and to the railway stations. Empty barrels were returned and washed in the cleansing shed. Malt, hops and sugar were carried to the brewhouse and coal was brought from the stockpile and shovelled into the boilers

to provide heat and steam. Spent grains and hops were carted away by farmers as feed and fertiliser. Coopers made and repaired casks in the cooperage, while carpenters, masons, slaters, plumbers, wheelwrights, farriers and their assorted assistants and apprentices maintained the brewery buildings and transport. Clerks carried the heavy leather-bound ledgers from the strong-room to the tall desks where all entries were made by hand with pen and ink. Messengers came with orders, while office boys ran to and from the city on errands. In the partners' offices the more elevated concerns of business were dealt with by James J. Murphy and his brothers.

Early Growth

James J. Murphy very quickly established a strong trade for its porter. Lady's Well Ale was brewed until 1861 but was discontinued with the departure of the company's head brewer of the time, Edward Lane. Porter was then the sole product until 1889 when Murphy's Stout was introduced.

Sales figures for the years 1858 to 1883 have survived (see Table 1) and show a spectacular rise from 22,725 barrels in 1858 to 42,990 barrels in 1861. Sales fell in the following year and this drop may be attributed to the difficulties caused by the loss of the services of Edward Lane and his successor's subsequent departure after only three months with the brewery. By 1864 trade was on the increase again and rose steadily to 96,676 barrels in 1872. Sales suffered occasional minor setbacks in the 1870s but by 1883 had risen to 119,112 barrels.

This steady growth is all the more impressive when it is realised that Cork city already had

Left: A steam train crossing the Chetwynd Viaduct on the West Cork Railway. The brewery relied on this and other railways radiating from Cork city to expand its trade.

three established breweries when James J. Murphy & Co. went into production. The Cork Porter Brewery of Beamish & Crawford had enjoyed the lion's share of the trade, but by 1859 it was felt that the Murphy brothers were serious competitors. In that year Richard Pigot Beamish wrote:

Our opponents the Murphys have succeeded in establishing a sale of some 40,000 tierces and have already captured one-third of our town customers. They are now proceeding to attack us in the country districts, and the result of the battle may be the necessity of a large expenditure of money.

The aggressive approach of the Murphys can be gauged from the military-type language of Beamish: 'captured', 'attack', 'battle'.

Reasons for Success

A number of factors combined to contribute to the early success of James J. Murphy & Co. The Great Famine of the 1840s was followed by a period of relative prosperity and the market for porter, amongst other products, began to grow steadily. Large and efficiently run breweries capable of meeting growing demand prospered. Lady's Well Brewery, though a little late in entering the fray, was well positioned for this growth.

The tastes of the drinking population changed during the nineteenth century. People turned away from spirits, partly due to higher prices for spirits resulting from increases in the taxes on distilling. Another factor in this change was the vigorous temperance campaign of the early decades of the century. While the total abstinence from all forms of alcoholic drink was the ultimate aim of the campaign, the drinking of porter and other beers was seen as less damaging than the consumption of spirits. The 'Apostle of

Fr Theobald Mathew, the 'Apostle of Temperance', who died in 1856.

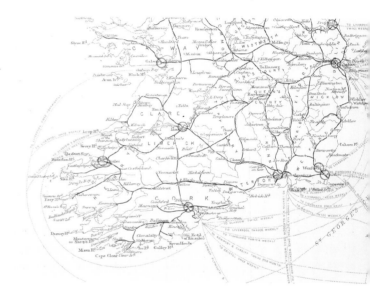

Right: Map showing the railway network that developed in Ireland in the 1800s. The railways were crucial to the growth of the brewery's trade in the south of Ireland.

Temperance', Father Theobald Mathew, died in Cork in 1856, the year Lady's Well Brewery was founded. The two events are unconnected but his passing led to a certain slackening in the energy of the temperance movement.

The 1800s also saw the growth of Ireland's railway network. This, coupled with an improvement in the quality of roads, facilitated the affordable transport of porter and other products to areas not previously accessible. During the middle decades of the century a number of railway lines were developed in Cork, radiating out from the city. The brewery used these to supply the county towns of Bandon, Bantry, Cobh, Macroom, Mallow, Passage, Youghal and many more. Sea transport was used to supply some coastal towns.

Trade was also secured through the acquisition of 'tied houses' (see highlight, pp. 118-121). These public houses were bought or otherwise acquired by the brewery and let to tenants who were obliged to deal only with James J. Murphy & Co. and to sell only its products.

While there was some variation in the nature of the 'tie', the system guaranteed an outlet for the brewery's porter. The brewery paid less than £200 for these public houses in most instances but they did represent a large and growing investment. By 1883, 104 public houses in the city and county were tied to the brewery. Over half of these premises were the property of the brewery while the others were obliged to trade because the licence belonged to the firm. These properties and their trade were valued at £116,500 in 1883. The brewery also supplied 'independent' or 'free' public houses.

The business skills of the Murphy brothers, learnt in the related trade of distilling, also played a part in the success of the brewery venture. The vision and dedication of the senior partner, James J., in particular, led the enterprise and positioned the brewery to take advantage of all opportunities for expansion of trade.

The Murphy name was well known in the commercial and political life of the city and the family had, for generations, been prominently associated with many charitable and religious causes. Positive associations such as these must have given a product with the Murphy name a certain measure of acceptance among the public. The fact that they were Catholic would have given them an advantage in a predominantly Catholic country; their main competitors, Beamish & Crawford and Guinness, were both Protestant owned. The employees of the company also played their part, of course, and brewed a porter the quality and flavour of which was of a sufficiently high standard to win over a large proportion of the city's drinkers within a relatively short period of time.

Profits

A barrel of porter sold for between 28s and 30s during the 1858-83 period and the profit per barrel varied, depending on the cost of raw materials, wages and other charges. The profit in the period ranged from 3s to 6s per barrel. (See illustration showing cost breakdown, p. 43.)

Between 1858 and 1883 James J. Murphy & Co. showed a profit every year except in 1872, 1874 and 1875. The profits were divided between the partners after all charges and running costs had been met. This nett profit was divided in proportion to the share held by each partner. Up to 1865 James J. and William received one-third of profits each and Jerome, Francis and Nicholas received one-ninth each. Under that arrangement the two principal partners earned between £726 10s 2d and £3,000 each per year, 1865 being the most profitable. In 1865 the partnership changed and from then on Nicholas received a fixed annual payment of £400, the remainder, if any, of his former one-ninth share went to the 'rest' or reserve account.

Losses of £4,200 and £3,416 and £121 were recorded in 1872, 1874 and 1875 respectively. Apart from those setbacks the partners did well from their shares of the profits. In 1869, for

£1 = 20s
1s = 12d

The division of the brewery's surplus in the year ending 31 October 1859.

example, a nett profit of £12,440 was made and the two principal partners' share was over £4,000 each, while the lesser partners earned almost £1,400 each.

From 1872 the profit-share system changed again: James J. and William received three-eighths each and Jerome and Francis received one-eighth each. The annual payment of £400 to Nicholas was charged before profits were divided.

In the late 1870s and in the years up to 1883 profits were quite substantial. Buoyant annual sales of 100,000 barrels were being recorded and nett profits reached £26,986 in 1879 on sales of over £140,000. In 1881 the profit was £33,080 on sales of over £160,000. The partners' shares of these profits were huge sums in the context of the period. In 1881, for example, the most profitable of those years, James J. and William each received £11,250 as their share of profits.

In addition to sharing this surplus, many of the partners' day-to-day expenses were met by the brewery. Detailed figures have survived for the years 1861 to 1868. James J. drew down amounts ranging from £1,236 to £2,782 per year in that period. Many of his house expenses were paid in this way. The annual rent of his home at Bellevue in Passage amounted to £100. Other charges on his home, paid by the brewery, included window sashes, timber, stone, tiles, gravel, carpets, blinds, various items of furniture

as well as coal and payments to masons, carpenters, plumbers, painters, gas fitters and a bell hanger. James J. also drew £40 per month for general house expenses. This later rose to £50. Wine, whiskey, ale and cigars were paid for and also annual subscriptions to sports' and gentlemen's clubs. His yearly ticket for the Cork, Blackrock and Passage railway was charged to the brewery as were subscriptions to the *Cork Examiner*, the *Cork Herald*, the *Daily Reporter*, the *London News* and the *Southern Reporter*. James J.'s many contributions to charitable causes are also listed in these accounts: the Lying-in Hospital, the Lancastrian School, the North Monastery School, SS Peter and Paul's Church building fund, St Patrick's Orphanage, the Sisters of Mercy, Sunday's Well and Monkstown churches as well as numerous payments to

43

families and individuals in distress. Share purchases in the Munster Bank and in the National Investment Company were also paid for.

William Murphy's spending from this source was somewhat more extravagant, ranging from £2,348 in 1862 to £3,615 in 1867. His expenses covered the same range as those of James J. The other partners also had many of their expenses paid by the firm but their amounts were generally below £1,000 per year. From 1869 Jerome and Francis were paid an annual salary of £400 as brewers, in addition to their expenses and shares of profits.

The combined amounts from shared profits and paid expenses came to quite significant sums and enabled the partners and their families to live very comfortable lives. The scale of these annual incomes can be gauged, when in 1881, for example, the total annual wage bill of the brewery was £6,956 5s, while in the same year the two principal partners earned £11,250 each from their shares of profits, exclusive of paid expenses. At this time there were between 150 and 200 people employed at the brewery.

Despite these huge earnings the Murphys were perceived by the public as fair and generous employers. Brewery workers in the city enjoyed better rates of pay than their counterparts in other industries. In addition many payments were made to cover the funeral expenses of workers and to former workers' families who had fallen on hard times.

Change in Status

In the early 1880s a number of privately-owned firms changed their status and opted to become joint stock companies with shareholders. James J. Murphy & Co. was, by this time, a very successful family firm, earning quite healthy profits, and some of the sons of the partners were now of age and experience to participate more fully in the running of the business. It was decided that the firm would become a limited company, James J. Murphy & Co. Ltd, on 31 December 1883. It was felt that this new status would more efficiently control the destiny of the concern and protect the interests of the now extended Murphy family.

Table 1

Barrels Sold, Sales Income and Profit 1858-1883

Year (ending 31 October)	Barrels Sold	Sales Income	Profit
1858	22,725	£ 35,138	£ 2,539
1859	33,927	£ 51,840	£ 4,484
1860	41,465	£ 64,143	£ 2,367
1861	42,990	£ 65,283	£ 2,179
1862	37,429	£ 26,887	£ 3,138
1863	39,108	£ 83,358	£ 4,361
1864	38,093	£ 59,754	£ 7,189
1865	41,306	£ 63,193	£ 9,000
1866	45,674	£ 70,404	£ 6,630
1867	c.50,000	£ 76,454	£ c3,000
1868	58,109	£ 88,106	£ 8,070
1869	66,225	£ 99,739	£ 12,440
1870	76,480	£ 114,616	£ 457
1871	92,123	£ 136,788	£10,960
1872	96,676	£ 142,377	(£ 4,200)†
1873	89,944	£ 132,382	£ 3,563
1874	89,369	£ 134,289	(£ 3,416)†
1875	99,706	£ 145,260	(£ 121)†
1876	100,675	£ 146,861	£ 21,405
1877	95,826	£ 140,310	£ 13,602
1878	105,433	£ 153,272	£ 21,521
1879	97,835	£ 143,805	£ 26,986
*1880	98,205	£ 144,283	£ 20,798
1881	110,111	£ 162,101	£ 33,080
1882	115,924	£ 170,790	£ 28,589
1883	119,112	£ 176,625	£ 25,843

*From this year the brewery year ended 30 September

† Losses

JAMES J. MURPHY

& Co. LIMITED.

LADYS WELL

BREWERY

4

The Glory Years

James J. Murphy & Co. was not alone in changing its status to that of a limited company during this period. In Cork, during the latter decades of the nineteenth century, quite a number of companies became incorporated and issued shares: nine in the 1870s; six in the 1880s; eighteen in the 1890s. During these years also almost every major brewery in Britain converted to limited liability status and issued shares.

Many of these new limited liability companies took company status but did not publicly market their shares. They were anxious to retain family control and were essentially private limited companies. In law there was no difference between them and public companies until 1908. In common with most brewery floatations, the equity in James J. Murphy & Co. Ltd was entirely retained by the original partners who became directors of the new company.

James J. Murphy & Co. Ltd

The new company had a share capital of £250,000 - 2,500 shares of £100. James J., the chairman of the new company, held 958 shares, his brothers William, Francis and Jerome held 926, 356 and 257 shares respectively. Albert St John, a son of James J., Henry, a son of William and another Jerome held one share each. In 1887, Charles Eustace, another son of James J., replaced the latter Jerome as a shareholder.

In 1888 James J. shed 101 of his shares and brought the holdings of his sons, Albert St John and Charles Eustace, to fifty each. Henry Noblett

(company solicitor), Richard Tivy (company secretary) and Edward Jones received one share each. William reduced his holding by 100 shares and his sons Captain (later Major) William and Harry had fifty and fifty-one shares respectively.

In 1889 William Murphy died and in addition to a distribution of his shares, the company issued 500 new £100 shares. This brought the issued share capital to £300,000. From May 1889 the breakdown of shareholdings was as follows:

James J. Murphy	1,032
Francis Murphy	427
Capt William Murphy (son of William)	360
Jerome Murphy	309
Harry Murphy (son of William)	272
Mrs Mary Nicholson (daughter of William)	180
Mrs Maude Foster (daughter of William)	180
Mrs William J. Murphy	120
Albert St John Murphy (son of James J.)	60
Charles Eustace Murphy (son of James J.)	60
Total	**3,000**

With the deaths of James J. in 1897, of Jerome in 1899 and of Francis in 1919 the shares were redistributed but essentially the Murphy family, much extended, retained virtually all shares until the 1960s.

Competition

James J. Murphy & Co. Ltd had three principal competitors in Cork city. These were Beamish & Crawford, Lane & Co. and Sir John Arnott & Co. Ltd. By the late 1880s James J. Murphy & Co. Ltd was the leading producer in Cork, brewing about 48 per cent of the city's output. Beamish & Crawford had about 27 per cent and the two other breweries about 12.5 per cent each. At the beginning of the twentieth century only two breweries remained in the city as James J. Murphy & Co. Ltd had taken over the firm of Sir John Arnott & Co. Ltd and Beamish & Crawford had taken over Lane & Co.

Guinness of Dublin was by then the biggest brewery in Great Britain and Ireland. It had grown to dominate the Irish market and had a significant presence in Britain and elsewhere. Guinness had not, however, managed to threaten the Cork breweries on their home ground. The tied house system, as operated by Murphy's and Beamish & Crawford, effectively protected them from succumbing to Guinness domination. Within the Cork region at this time the greatest competition was between the two larger local breweries.

Brewery Expansion

In the late 1880s the company decided to expand, remodel and upgrade the brewery. This was necessary to give greater capacity and to take full advantage of improvements in brewing technology. In 1889 £50,000 was raised through the issue of 500 new £100 shares and this funded much of the new building costs. Between October 1889 and September 1892 about £72,000 was spent on this work.

Malt House

A new malt house was built at a cost of £4,640 in what became known as the lower or southern courtyard. It was stone built, had five floors and was 'of handsome elevation'. Two floors were used for storing barley and the other three were malt floors. At the northern end of the building was a metal steep. This was where the barley was steeped to encourage germination. From there the barley was brought to the malt floors before being dried in the kilns. Two kilns were located at the southern end of the malt house and heat was provided by Free's furnaces. The barley and malt were moved on a system of elevators.

The malt house, completed in 1889. Malting took place between October and May, so the malt workers were seasonal employees. Most were from rural areas and returned to the country to work on the harvest when the malt season was completed. Up until the Second World War the 'malt gang' lived on the premises. Their day began at 6 a.m. and continued until 5.30 p.m. They resumed at 9 p.m. with the night-time duty of 'dragging' the floors. The company had another maltings in Riverstown outside Cork city and later aquired malt houses on Devonshire Street and John Street, close to the brewery.

The building was designed by T. Hynes FRIBA and at the time was said to have been 'built and arranged on the newest principle and fitted throughout with the latest appliances known to modern science'. The malt house still stands and was remodelled in the early 1990s and converted to office use.

Mill House and Brewhouse

In the upper or northern courtyard a new mill house was built on to the front of the brewhouse and both those buildings were newly fitted out. New rollers by the firm of Robert Ganz were installed in the mill house to crush the malt prior to mashing. New screens 'of the barrel kind' by Nalder & Co. of Wantage screened the malt. Two new mash tuns, with a capacity of 500 and 300 barrels, from the firm of William Spence of Dublin, were installed, along with new elevators and grist hoppers. Iron floors were built to take the new machinery and iron stairways were put in between the floors. New Warsham heaters, wort coppers and hop backs completed the fitting out of these buildings.

Racking cellar, where casks were filled.

Cooling House

A new cooling house was built at a cost of £4,304 and seven Morton refrigerators were used to cool the wort prior to fermentation. Advances had been made in the science of refrigeration and an ammonia plant by Pontifex and Wood was built. A visitor to the brewery in 1895 wrote: 'The Lady's Well Brewery is the only one in Ireland, except Guinness, where this expensive and modern plant is to be found.'

New fermenting tuns of oak were built by T. R. Carty and the tun room where they were located was described in a newspaper account of 1892 as 'lofty and capacious, and the huge iron-hooped tuns that cover its floor have between them a capacity of 2,560 barrels'.

There were four cleansing houses in the remodelled brewery, with six settling squares and three sets of cleansing rounds, all of oak. The settling-tank house had two huge slate settling tanks each with a 570 barrel capacity. The vat house was on the floor above the racking cellar and held eight vats.

Racking Cellar

The racking cellar was, according to a visitor,

. . . a sight that amazed us. Branching right and left were seen long alleys and avenues extending many hundreds of feet, running between a forest of casks, which at the lowest computation must have numbered many thousands, of porter maturing for thirsty Irishmen.

Mr Roche, an engineer employed at the brewery, had patented a cock to aid the filling of casks. The brewery was quite proud, as ever, of another technical improvement:

The nozzle of the cock when placed in the bunghole of the cask is rendered perfectly air-

tight by an India-rubber band becoming securely wedged. The air rushing up the tube drives all the froth back to the racking vessel and when the pure liquor shows itself in the glass indicator it is immediately apparent that the cask is now filled to its utmost capacity.

Cask Cleansing Shed

Over £9,000 was spent on the new cask cleansing shed and on its new boilers, chimney shaft and machinery. Up to 1,500 casks per day could be washed. Hot water and chains were used to wash the insides of the casks and they were then dried using blowers of hot and cold air. All machinery was 'of the newest pattern and . . . with such splendid arrangements it is practically impossible for a sour cask to be transmitted to any customer'. Indeed, a 'nose', a man whose function it was to smell every cask, was employed in this area to ensure the cleanliness of every cask before it was passed to the racking cellar.

Electric Power

A tall chimney shaft was built at the cask cleansing shed where two steel boilers by Adamson of Hyde and a horizontal engine by

Cask cleansing shed, built in the early 1890s at a cost of over £9,000.

Roby of Lincoln were located. This engine also worked the elevators of the adjacent malt house and a dynamo which lit the southern parts of the brewery. Further electrical power was provided by a combined turbine and dynamo by Parsons, which was located in the northern courtyard. In 1890 £1,321 was spent on an 'Electric Light Installation' and £816 was spent the following year. In 1892 a new turbine dynamo was

Electrical house. The brewery generated all of its own electricity needs until 1916. Electricity was principally used for lighting and to power grain elevators.

Right: Lady's Well Brewery in 1890. While much rebuilding had been completed, the new offices and entrance gateway had yet to be built. (Compare with the 1906 view of the brewery, p. 71.)

purchased for £500. The brewery was by now electrically lit throughout and the commitment to this power source continued when an 'electric generating house, of considerable dimensions' was built a few years later to supply all the electricity needs of the brewery.

Safety

A steam fire-pump, 'capable of sending 12,000 gallons of water per hour to the most distant part of the works' was installed in the centre of the upper courtyard. Accounts of the time praise the company for its attention to safety. 'A Government inspector has declared that this brewery is one of the best protected factories in the Kingdom' wrote the *Daily Independent* in 1892. Another account added that 'it is not until one has seen the numerous precautions taken for the safety of the employees that the justice of the observation is fully felt'.

each stall. In the early 1890s the place of honour 'under the clock' was given to a horse called Swiper.

The draymen took great pride in the health and appearance of their horses. A visitor to Cork city in 1895 remarked:

. . . the streets of the city are made bright by the gleaming harness and glossy coats of the Lady's Well horses penetrating every nook and corner of the town under the guidance of their well-clad and comfortable draymen.

The draymen wore white smocks or aprons. A 1902 guide to the brewery wrote:

These sturdy draymen are a fine set of fellows, and not only do their ruddy faces betoken good health, but their sleek condition testifies to the wholesomeness of Murphy's porter.

New Offices

The building of the new offices was begun in December 1892 when the remodelling of the brewery proper was almost completed. The offices were designed by the architectural firm of Hynes of Cork and the builders were Messrs E. and P. O'Flynn of Watercourse Road, Cork. A new brewery entrance, flanking the northern side of the offices, was also built. The gates were of wrought iron and the piers of cut limestone. Over

The new stables, built in 1890, were located on Leitrim Street, across from the brewery.

Stables

New stables were built opposite the brewery on Leitrim Street. There were twenty-four 'excellently equipped' stalls and an enamelled shield, bearing each horse's name, hung over

the main gateway the legend 'Lady's Well Brewery Co. Ltd' was executed in wrought iron as was the coat of arms of Cork which was a registered trademark of James J. Murphy & Co. Ltd. A correspondent of the *Wine Merchant and Grocer's Review* in 1895 remarked as follows on the new offices:

No expense has been spared, and the offices are the most magnificent of their kind in the country . . . There are no brewery offices in Ireland at all as handsome as these offices of Murphy's.

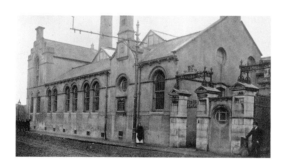

On the counter in the public office was an eight foot high screen of cut glass. This was divided into three and the coat of arms of the Murphy family was engraved on the central panel, while the arms of Cork and of the province of Munster decorated the other two. There were three waiting rooms off the public office and the building also contained a counting house, a boardroom, a cashier's and auditor's room, directors' private rooms, the secretary's office, a strongroom, stationery stores and the office of the chairman James J. Murphy. The *Wine Merchant and Grocer's Review* stated:

Mr Murphy's room is perhaps the smallest apartment in the building and, while furnished with everything requisite, speaks eloquently of the unselfish disposition of the distinguished Cork man, who has founded the largest industrial concern in his native city.

The building was furnished to the highest office standards of the time. A system of speaking tubes formed 'complete intercommunication between the departments'. All rooms were heated by Sharland's Manchester grates. Electric lights were installed by G. Percival of Cork and there was a telephone in the main office. The local firm of Lynch brothers provided the furniture, 'which in all details evidences the warm and practical interest in local industry, characteristic of the firm'. The brewery was also quite proud of the new office lavatories. These adjoined the boardroom and were 'of the most commodious and modern kind, replete with the latest sanitary appliances'.

The new malt house, brewery buildings and offices were the pride of the firm and a very visible testament to the growing commercial success of James J. Murphy & Co. Ltd. Correspondents of newspapers, trade journals and commercial directories from both Britain and Ireland enjoyed the hospitality of the brewery, praised its innovation and success and were optimistic for its future. Annual output was approaching 130,000 barrels when the following was written:

Left: Exterior of the brewery offices, built in 1892-3. Only the facade survives.

Interior of the brewery offices.

Ledgers from the
Murphy Brewery
archive.

*[James J. Murphy & Co. Ltd] alone has risen
above the level of the lesser breweries, and has
taken a stand on a plane by itself at a
measurable and constantly decreasing distance
from [Guinness] while in the City of Cork and the
greater part of the province of Munster it outstrips
all competitors without any exception.*

Porter and Stout

In addition to beginning the remodelling of the
brewery in 1889, that year also saw the
introduction of stout as a new product. It was
first brewed in May. Murphy's Stout was
stronger than its porter. The stout had an original
gravity (strength) of 1072. This stout was known
as Double or XX Stout and was said to be
'somewhat fuller and stronger [than porter], a

generous pleasant drink, which we found to be a
potent tipple'. Murphy's Porter had a gravity of
1056. A Single or X Stout was also sold from
1889. This was a blend of 80 per cent porter and
20 per cent stout and had a gravity of 1060.

Murphy's Stout quickly established a
market and accounted for between 20 and 25 per
cent of sales income between 1890 and 1905. In
the absence of precise records it is not possible
to establish exact figures for barrels of stout sold.
In the 1890s an average of 13,500 barrels of stout
were brewed each year. Some was sold as XX
Stout but a proportion was blended with porter
and sold as X Stout. The brewery records that
survive for those years only give the income from
stout sales, without distinguishing between XX
Stout and X Stout, and do not note the number of

barrels sold. Total barrelage (stout and porter combined) has been relatively accurately established up to 1900 (See Table 2). Some references in brewery ledgers suggest that X Stout was the bigger seller. In 1890, for example, sales of X Stout were almost three times greater than those of XX Stout.

The brewery was very proud of its stout and porter and was not averse to promoting the medicinal value of its brews. A visitors' guide to the brewery, published in 1902, stated that 'porter is acknowledged by the medical profession to be a most nourishing drink when taken in moderation', and 'we also tested some invalid stout, a beverage highly recommended by doctors for its powerful tonic properties, and for which the firm is famous'.

The newspapers and trade journals of the period also praised the quality of Murphy's Stout. The *Cork Herald* noted in 1892:
In their newly developed stout trade the firm has shown a readiness to couch a lance against all comers in order that the public palate may have an opportunity of testifying to the health-giving properties of Murphy's XX.

An article in the *Daily Independent* in the

We also tested some invalid stout, a beverage highly recommended by doctors for its powerful tonic properties, and for which the firm is famous.

same year stated: 'Those who have tasted Murphy's stout declare it to be equal, if not superior to that brewed by any other firm in Ireland'. One of the directors of the company was quoted as saying: 'We do not hope to thrive on pushing and puffing; our sole grounds for seeking popular favour is the excellence of our product.' Two outside 'experts' gave their verdicts on the new stout. A Sir Charles Cameron said: 'I am satisfied that this stout has been skilfully brewed from malt and hops only, and those of the best quality', and one Dr Hassel of London was equally complimentary, saying: 'It can be pronounced to be of very good quality.'

Taste Tests

In 1895 a correspondent of the *Wine Merchant and Grocer's Review* visited the brewery in the company of a wine merchant. The wine merchant was sceptical of the quality of Murphy's Stout and thought himself quite a connoisseur of

Left: The main brewery gateway in 1900.

stouts. The account continues:

'I can tell G_____'s stout at once. I take a bottle of stout every day for my dinner, and I would know G_____'s anywhere', said my friend. Whereupon the energetic secretary produced a bottle of Murphy's double stout and a bottle of G_____'s double stout. The wine merchant was requested to leave the room, and in the writer's presence, Mr Tivy opened both bottles and poured the contents of each into a separate glass. Then the wine merchant was permitted to re-enter the room, and was requested to say which of the two stouts he preferred. The bottles had, of course, been concealed under the table. Our friend began to smell and taste, and at length, taking up the glass of Murphy's in his hand, he exclaimed with great emphasis: 'This is G_____'s, I'd know it anywhere!'

We laughed heartily at his mistake and his confusion will be likely to result in his conversion.

The writer then declared his ability to distinguish Guinness from Murphy's. Having chosen Murphy's, declaring it to be Guinness, 'a loud explosion of laughter from the audience greeted his declaration . . . Despite all my study, all I know is that I know nothing.'

Another group, visiting the brewery in 1902, tasted the stout and their remarks were noted as follows:

Programme entry for the 1892 Dublin Distillers' and Brewers' Exhibition.

'Hum, by Jove, this is stout!' Another, 'Why, this is admirable!' Another, 'This is exquisite!' After this we became hearty and cheerful, and in a lively humour for our further peregrinations.

Medals for Stout

In August 1892 the first Distillers', Brewers' and Allied Trades Exhibition was held at the Rotunda in Dublin. The aim of the exhibition was to

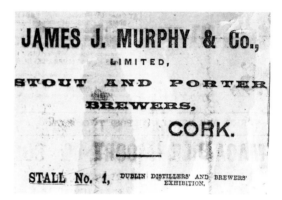

further the interests of the drinks industry in Ireland by presenting the best of Irish whiskey, stout, ale and mineral waters and by showing machinery and fittings related to their manufacture and sale. James J. Murphy & Co. Ltd took a stand at the exhibition which was described in a contemporary newspaper account:

There there is displayed, and can be sampled, the celebrated double stout of the Lady's Well Brewery, and the tasteful arrangement reflects the

The medals won by Murphy's Stout in Dublin (1892) and in Manchester (1895), which still feature on Murphy's Irish Stout labels.

55

highest credit upon Mr Tivy, the company's popular and energetic secretary, who personally supervised its erection. Messrs Murphy are most anxious that the trade should avail of this opportunity to test and compare their stout with that of any other firm.

Murphy's Double Stout was awarded the exhibition diploma and medal in the bottled stout and ale section. Three years later, in 1895, Murphy's Stout again took the supreme award for stout at the Brewers and Allied Trades Exhibition in Manchester. Both these medals are displayed on the present Murphy's Irish Stout labels.

Trade in Ireland and Abroad

James J. Murphy & Co. was keen to capitalise on the favourable notices its stout was receiving in the early 1890s. By 1892 it was enjoying 'a large and increasing trade' in Belfast through Messrs Brydon & Co. Neither was it afraid of taking on Guinness, the Goliath of the stout trade in Ireland and abroad, in Dublin, its home turf: 'Nay, even in Dublin, that ground so long sacred, so consecrated to the worship of a great name, Murphy's stout is on sale at some of the leading restaurants.' Agencies were set up in Limerick, Kilmallock, Tralee and Waterford, as well as in the larger County Cork towns.

The brewery also established an export trade for its stout. A commercial directory from the period wrote:

With characteristic enterprise Messrs Murphy have opened up a trade in the colonies, London, Manchester, South Wales and other parts of England, in all of which places their productions have been most favourably received.

The firm maintained an agency in London, where Mr Joseph Nolan looked after its interests.

The *Brewers' Journal* of 15 November 1892 wrote: *[Murphy's stout] is now to be had in many restaurants in the metropolis and elsewhere. It possesses a rich flavour, and is bottled in splendid condition; this firm bids fair before long to command a portion of the stupendous trade for Irish stout, which has hitherto been almost monopolized by the great Dublin brewery.*

The company balance sheet for 1892 notes that the London agency was holding twenty-three hogsheads of stout, worth £78 15s, as well as £238 9s 7d worth of bottled stout. Presumably the stout was being exported in bulk and bottled in London.

The company also had offices in Manchester and Bolton in England and in Newport in Wales. Detail on these offices in the brewery records is scanty with no information as to their volume of trade. Mr William Cuffe was in charge of the Manchester operation and conducted business until April 1916, when it was decided to close it due to the difficulties caused by the war. However, it would seem that the office opened again after the war, as an entry in a Directors' Minute Book for 4 May 1923 shows it to be then functioning. It was also decided to close the Newport agency in 1916 but Mr N. G. Sutton, the agent, visited the brewery and succeeded in persuading the directors to reverse their decision. The Bolton agency, run by Mr J. H. Stirrup, does not appear to have been as successful as the others. It was closed in August 1908.

Bottle label from the 1890s.

In 1892 'energetic agents and travellers' also attempted to establish a trade in the United States of America. The *Cork Herald* of 25 June of that year wrote:

New ground has also been opened up in America, and those of our exiled kith and kin in that country will be in a position to sip of the creamy stout brewed within sight and within sound of some of the most historic scenes of their boyhood's years.

The American operation seems not to have met with great success. There is no reference to that trade in any of the brewery records and in the absence of such information it may be concluded that the venture was not pursued for too long a period.

Science and Barley

In the later nineteenth century a number of advances were made in the scientific aspects of brewing. This was especially so in the matter of brewing yeasts. The work of Louis Pasteur and others had the effect of convincing breweries that investment in laboratories and attention to the microbiological details of the brewing process paid dividends by improving quality. In Lady's Well Brewery the laboratory was located near the head brewer's office and was 'furnished and fitted with the usual apparatus'. This included 'a complete set of Pasteurising trays, microscopes, and the subsidiary testing vessels all showing that nothing is overlooked to maintain the reputation for the quality of their beers'.

It was also realised in those years that the quality of malt and of the barley used for malting was crucial to the brewing of top quality stout and porter. In the late 1880s Guinness, in association with the Irish Agricultural Organisation Society, undertook experiments in barley growing to promote the cultivation of grains more suitable to malting and of improved quality. James J. Murphy & Co. Ltd also saw the benefits of improved barley quality and they too took measures to improve the cultivation of good malting barley. Selected seed was imported and supplied to farmers at cost price. By 1902 the firm had 'succeeded in raising the standard of malting barley throughout the district'.

Most of the barley used at the brewery was grown in County Cork, one of the best barley-growing counties in Ireland. By 1901 Lady's Well Brewery had become the biggest brewer in the southern region and its purchases of barley were an important element in the agricultural economy of the area. The quantity of malt used at the brewery grew from 33,602 barrels in 1884 to a high of 76,497 barrels in 1902.

In the decades prior to 1884 the price of malt never fell below 23s per barrel. In the later 1880s and 1890s the price was lower, generally below 20s per barrel.

During the 1890s about 10,000 barrels of barley were malted at the brewery each year, and most of the remaining requirement was malted by the concerns of D. Redmond, the Cork Malting Company and by D. Donegan & Sons. The brewery also had a grain store close by on Devonshire Street where barley was dried before being sent for malting to the brewery malt house or to Donegan's malt house on John Street, on the western side of the brewery. In 1909 the brewery purchased Donegan's malt house for £4,056. Eight years previously, in 1901, another malt house had been acquired at Riverstown when the brewery took over the firm of Sir John Arnott & Co. Ltd.

SIR JOHN ARNOTT AND ST FIN BARRE'S BREWERY

John Arnott was born in Scotland in 1814 and arrived in Cork in 1835 'to seek his fortune'. In this he succeeded and became prominent in the business and political life of the city. He resided at Woodlands, 'a princely residence' in the Montenotte area, and was knighted in 1859 on the occasion of laying the foundation stone of the new Patrick's Bridge in Cork, the old one having been swept away by floods. This was during the first of his three terms as Lord Mayor of the city; he also served as Liberal MP for Kinsale between 1859 and 1861. Among his business endeavours were the Cork Park racecourse; a bakery in the city; shops in Cork and Dublin (Arnott's department store went on to become one of the major retail outlets in Dublin); and the *Irish Times* newspaper, which he purchased in 1873. His connection with brewing began a decade previously when he purchased Abbot's Brewery in Cork.

Abbot's Brewery had been established in 1805 and originally brewed a sweet table beer called 'Abbot's Beer'. It was taken over in

1861 by Sir John Arnott & Co. Ltd, overhauled and remodelled, and renamed St Fin Barre's Brewery on account of its location, on Fitton Street, now Sharman Crawford Street, near St Fin Barre's Cathedral. Porter and stout were brewed there, while ale was produced at the company's other brewery in Riverstown, outside the city. Arnott's did an extensive trade in the British army canteens in the south of Ireland, as well as in Belfast and the major British cities. The Mediterranean stations of the army were also supplied, while the company exported in considerable quantities to the West Indies and had branch offices in Barbados, Demerara and St Thomas.

Arnott's employed around 150 at its height in the 1870s, and had an extensive tied house estate. One of its claims to fame was that the first steam engine put up in Cork was a beam engine made for the St Fin Barre's brewery.

Arnott's thrived in its first three decades, and in the 1870s and 1880s was producing approximately 12.5 per cent of the beer brewed in the city. However, it went into decline in the 1890s and following the death of Sir John Arnott in 1898 its decline became terminal. It was taken over as a non-

operational concern by James J. Murphy & Co. Ltd in 1901. (In the same year Beamish & Crawford's took over the city's only other brewery, Lane's on South Main Street.)

In March 1901 the Murphy's board issued £50,000 worth of debentures to raise funds for the purchase of Arnott's. In the following month the company paid over £80,750 for St Fin Barre's Brewery, Riverstown Ale Brewery and malt house, and Arnott's tied house estate of approximately 150 pubs. The premises of the St Fin Barre's brewery were sold in 1903 to two companies, the Cork and Kerry Creamery Co. and Shanahan & Co., and in 1906 the site was levelled for the building of a new technical school. The site of the old St Fin Barre's Brewery of Sir John Arnott & Co. is today occupied by the Crawford College of Art and Design and St Aloysius school for girls.

Inscription, St Patrick's Bridge, Cork.

The West Cork Bottling Co. Ltd

In 1896 James J. Murphy & Co. Ltd set up a subsidiary company, the West Cork Bottling Co. Ltd. This new company bottled and distributed Murphy's stout and porter and looked after brewery interests in the western parts of the county. It manufactured mineral waters and imported and distributed wines and spirits also. The West Cork Bottling Co. Ltd was based in Bandon, about twenty miles from Cork city, and had its own agents and stores in most of the towns of west Cork. It was a profitable and well-run enterprise and was, according to Albert St John Murphy, 'a great aid to us in putting our stout before the public in the best possible condition, both draught and in bottle'. (See highlight, pp. 60-61.)

Zenith

James J. Murphy & Co. Ltd enjoyed great success in the years from 1884 to 1905. Sales increased steadily throughout the period and profits were always healthy. The brewery was extended and rebuilt in the early 1890s and in the following years the addition of new capacity and the updating of facilities continued. New products were launched and the firm embarked on an export drive. A subsidiary company was established in 1896 and in 1901 the brewing firm of Sir John Arnott & Co. Ltd was taken over. Arnott's St Fin Barre's Brewery on Fitton Street in the city and its ale brewery at Riverstown were closed down but its estate of tied houses was added to Murphy's own. Murphy's now had almost 200 tied public houses, mostly in the city, which consolidated its trade. The numbers employed at the brewery grew to about 200 and the annual wage bill rose from £6,209 in 1884 to almost £15,000 in 1905. As an employer the firm was ' looked up to and trusted by a large staff and their fair dealing to their employees is as remarkable as their brew is excellent'.

The success of the firm in those years was greatly aided by the esteem in which the Murphy family was held in Cork. It was said that 'in the mouths of their fellow citizens their name has long been a synonym for a generosity and open-handedness'. James J. Murphy was seen as 'one of the brightest examples the South of Ireland affords of enterprise and commercial ability'. The Munster Bank rescue of 1885, led by James J. Murphy, and the great publicity generated by the presentations to him in 1890 by grateful citizens kept the Murphy name and that of the brewery before the public. As the fiftieth anniversary of Lady's Well Brewery approached in 1906, James J. Murphy & Co. Ltd was Ireland's second biggest brewer (after Guinness, which was one of the world's largest). The golden jubilee would afford an opportunity for the celebration of its achievement.

WEST CORK BOTTLING CO. LTD

This company was set up as a wholly-owned subsidiary of James J. Murphy & Co. Ltd in 1896 and had a share capital of £4,000. This was made up of 400 £10 shares and they were held by shareholders of the parent company. The board of the West Cork Bottling Co. Ltd was always chaired by the chairman of James J. Murphy & Co. Ltd, beginning with James J. Murphy himself. The new company was based in Bandon, some twenty miles from Cork, and had its offices, plant and stores on Deal Yard Lane. These buildings now serve as the Bandon Fire Station.

Mr Joseph Brennan was appointed company secretary and managed the affairs of the new concern for the following fifty years. Prior to 1896, he had been an agent for the brewery in west Cork, had bottled its products and had built up a large trade in the region. The area serviced by the West Cork Bottling Co. Ltd stretched from Kinsale, in the east, to Allihies, on the tip of the Beara peninsula, in the west

and included many remote towns, villages and offshore islands that could not effectively have been served from Cork. The success of the company in its first fifty years can be largely attributed to the work of Joseph Brennan.

The company had agents and stores in Kinsale, Dunmanway, Skibbereen, Schull, Castletownbere and Macroom. Murphy's Stout and Porter were bottled and distributed from Bandon, as were wines and spirits. Mineral waters and fruit cordials were manufactured also and supplied to the brewery's tied houses.

During the First World War agricultural produce was fetching a very high price and there was a significant increase in spending power in rural areas. The company did exceptionally well in those years and built up strong reserves.

The years of the independence struggle and civil war (1919-1923) greatly disrupted the affairs of the West Cork Bottling Co. Ltd. Transport and

distribution were interfered with as road and railway bridges were destroyed. Public houses closed early and political unrest and military activity curtailed the economic and social life of the region. Trade and profits fell. In June 1922 fire destroyed most of the plant, two lorries and a store containing bottles and cases.

In the late 1920s and into the following decade the Irish economy was in a depressed state. Trading conditions were poor, but despite this the company made profits. The Second World War brought new difficulties. Transport was affected as fuel was rationed. Spirits were also rationed and the importation of wines and raw materials for mineral water manufacture was disrupted. However, the Bandon operation 'gave satisfactory and gratifying returns', according to the chairman of the board.

Joseph Brennan died in 1948 and was succeeded by his son, Thomas. He died suddenly only three years later and his son, Joseph, took over the running of the firm. During the mid-1950s much expenditure was incurred in modernising and renewing the plant and in expanding the transport fleet. In 1957 Arthur Masson took over from Joseph Brennan. Profits increased and healthy dividends were paid to the brewery every year up to the mid-1960s. A new brand of minerals, 'Spring', was introduced and was extremely successful.

The later 1960s saw a decline in the fortunes of the company. Market conditions were changing and competition came from new sources with the growth of cash-and-carry outlets and supermarkets. The parent company's partnership with Watney-Mann, while initially fruitful, had later

soured and James J. Murphy & Co. Ltd was saved from liquidation by Taiscí Stáit, the state business rescue agency, in 1971.

In 1974 the Licensed Vintners Co-Operative Society Ltd took over the brewery and its subsidiary. A new bottling plant was built in Cork and this and other rationalisation measures effectively wound down the West Cork Bottling Co. Ltd. It survived in name only and following the 1982-3 receivership of the parent company

and its subsequent acquisition by Heineken, it was bought by Frank Wood Wolfe and Gerald Donovan.

The new West Cork Bottling Co. is now based in Skibbereen. Though no longer engaged in bottling, it is one of the largest distributors of Murphy Brewery Ireland Ltd products.

Table 2			
Year	**Barrels Sold**	**Sales Income**	**Profit**
1884	122,410	£176,136	£32,171
1885	112,875	£160,895	£33,796
1886	95,098	£137,029	£25,198
1887	91,726	£131,025	£25,596
1888	91,363	£132,173	£28,637
1889	101,614	£142,084	£29,514
1890	c.108,000	£159,232	£34,251
1891	108,637	£158,980	£32,297
1892	c.111,000	£162,309	£26,023
1893	c.118,000	£173,289	£23,125
1894	c.125,000	£180,215	£23,097
1895	c.125,000	£179,733	£25,537
1896	c.126,000	£182,352	£31,477
1897	c.126,000	£181,069	£23,482
1898	c.132,000	£189,687	£25,723
1899	c.135,000	£192,093	£21,954
*1900	140,000+	£250,062	£31,708
1901	?	£229,596	?
1902	?	£237,038	£30,542
1903	?	£228,533	£30,632
1904	?	£227,064	£22,911
1905	?	£222,317	£21,148

Barrels Sold, Sales Income and Profit 1884-1905

*From this year the brewery year ended 31 December instead of 30 September. Therefore 1900 figures are for fifteen months.

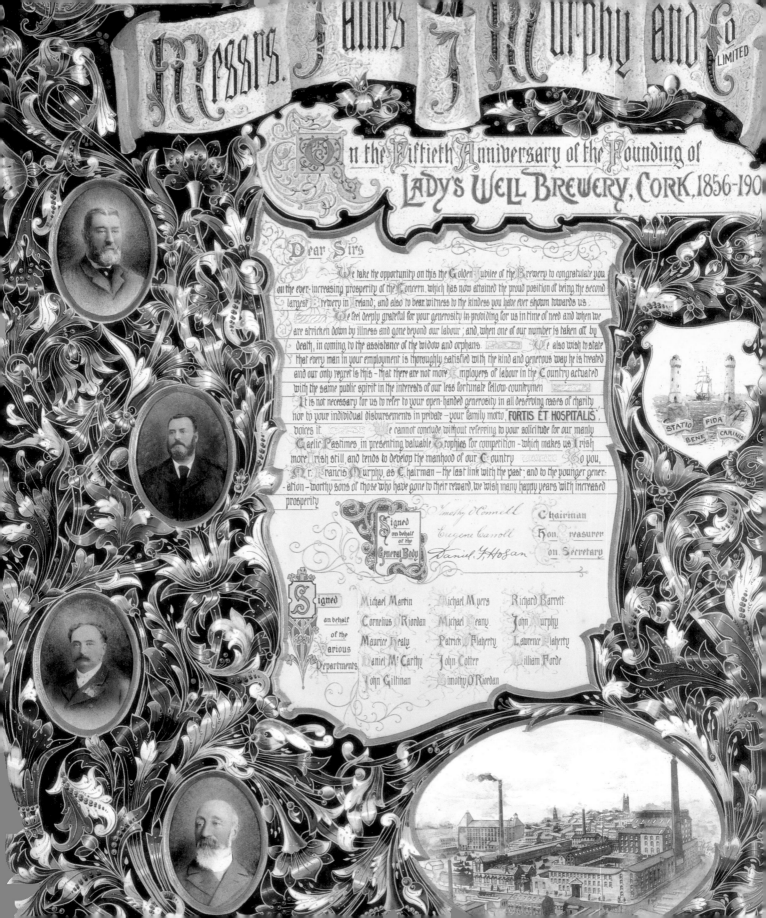

Messrs. James J. Murphy and Co. Limited

On the Fiftieth Anniversary of the Founding of Lady's Well Brewery, Cork, 1856-190[6]

Dear Sirs

We take the opportunity on this the Golden Jubilee of the Brewery to congratulate you on the ever-increasing prosperity of the Concern, which has now attained the proud position of being the second largest Brewery in Ireland; and also to bear witness to the kindness you have ever shown towards us. We feel deeply grateful for your generosity in providing for us in time of need and when we are stricken down by illness and gone beyond our labour; and, when one of our number is taken off by death, in coming to the assistance of the widow and orphans. We also wish to state that every man in your employment is thoroughly satisfied with the kind and generous way he is treated and our only regret is this — that there are not more Employers of labour in the Country actuated with the same public spirit in the interests of our less fortunate fellow-countrymen. It is not necessary for us to refer to your open-handed generosity in all deserving cases of charity nor to your individual disbursements in private — your family motto, "FORTIS ET HOSPITALIS", voices it. We cannot conclude without referring to your solicitude for our manly Gaelic Pastimes, in presenting valuable Trophies for competition — which makes us Irish more Irish still, and tends to develop the manhood of our Country. To you, Mr. Francis Murphy, as Chairman — the last link with the past; and to the younger generation — worthy sons of those who have gone to their reward, we wish many happy years with increased prosperity.

Signed on behalf of the General Body

Timothy O'Connell — Chairman
Eugene Carroll — Hon. Treasurer
Daniel F. Hogan — Hon. Secretary

Signed on behalf of the Various Departments

Michael Martin	Michael Myers	Richard Barrett
Cornelius O'Riordan	Michael Leany	John Murphy
Maurice Healy	Patrick O'Flaherty	Lawrence Flaherty
Daniel McCarthy	John Cotter	William Forde
John Giltinan	Timothy O'Riordan	

STATIO FIDA BENE CARINIS

From Golden Jubilee to Eve of War

The period from the golden jubilee to the First World War was relatively prosperous for the brewery, considering the poor economic climate in which it was operating. This period marked a low point in Cork's industrial history; between 1890 and the outbreak of war the city had lost two breweries, five tanneries, four engineering works, a gunpowder plant and many smaller firms. The situation in the countryside was not much better, and the lack of money in circulation and emigration affected all aspects of trade. During these years also, the region suffered a number of particularly harsh winters, which hit the brewery in the areas of raw materials and trade. Despite all of this, James J. Murphy & Co. Ltd continued to develop and modernise the plant at Lady's Well, improve the quality of its stout (the demand for which began to grow as that for porter declined in this period), and maintain its sales. The company steadily built up its capital reserves, from £19,000 in 1906 to £50,000 in 1913.

Golden Jubilee

In 1906 James J. Murphy & Co. Ltd celebrated the fiftieth anniversary of the founding of Lady's Well Brewery, and a number of events and presentations took place to mark the golden jubilee. On the Monday of the June Bank Holiday weekend the entire workforce was brought by train on a one-day excursion to Killarney, County Kerry at a cost of £259 17s 4d (see pp. 69-71). Such excursions by rail were a major feature of

Illuminated presentation from the staff to the directors marking the golden jubilee of Lady's Well Brewery, 1906.

life in many breweries throughout Britain and Ireland in this period. They were major recreational occasions for the employees who, it must be remembered, worked six days a week and did not have any paid annual holidays. The employees commissioned an ornate illuminated address from the celebrated firm of Gilbert and presented it to the board. It featured, along with fine words of praise for the directors, portraits of James J. Murphy and his three brothers, Francis, William and Jerome, the founders of the company, a painting of Lady's Well Brewery, and the Cork coat of arms, which was also a registered trademark of the company. The address was placed in a frame which was topped with the Murphy coat of arms. It still hangs in the brewery, as does a silver shield presented by the staff to mark the same occasion.

'A most trying year'

Despite the celebrations, 1906 was, in terms of trade, 'a most trying year' for the brewery. In addition to slowness of trade due to the shortage of spending power arising from the poor economic climate in the region, there was a huge increase in the price which the brewery had to pay for hops. Sales dropped by 4,000 barrels in the following year, largely due to the very bad weather and bad harvest. The principal losses were in the countryside, where the continuing drain of 'emigration from our shores' was having a negative effect on sales also. City sales, in contrast, improved in the second half of the year, despite the bad weather and 'the dearth of employment' there. The increase was especially noticeable in the stout trade, and was attributed by the chairman to the improved quality of the product to which much attention had been given in the preceding years. 'Our stout', the chairman was pleased to announce, 'is holding its own well and growing in favour slowly but surely with the public.'

The brewery sold far more beer (approximately double) in rural areas than in Cork city, but the city trade was more lucrative due to the lower costs of transport and commission. Overall profits were down in 1907 because of the drop in sales, increased costs related to plant maintenance and extension of the vatting facilities, and the continuing high price being paid for hops and coal. These losses, however, were partially offset by the lowering of the price of malt.

The Growing Popularity of Stout

The annual chairman's report for the year 1908 was delivered by Albert St John Murphy. The chairman, Francis Murphy was on a visit to Rome in early 1909, where he apparently enjoyed 'the confidence of the Holy Father'. The acting chairman was happy to report that the figures for the preceding year were 'eminently satisfactory . . . especially so in view of the dullness of the times and I may add the general stagnation of trade'.

Overall, output was slightly down on 1907 (by 869 barrels) but stout sales were up in both city and county. This marked an intensification of the trend of the previous couple of years during which public taste was moving 'decidedly in the stout direction'. Since 1905 the brewery had been producing a XXX Stout (discontinued in 1916) in addition to X and XX, while, since the turn of the century, increasing attention was being given to the scientific aspects of brewing and to efforts to improve the product and achieve 'that finished and clean flavour possessed by Guinness'. A Dr Moritz, a scientist who acted as a brewing consultant to Guinness among others, was brought in on a number of occasions to offer expert advice. New personnel were installed in the laboratory and brewing department in 1905 and in that year also the brewery directors with responsibility for the laboratories (John and Fitzjames Murphy) had been heavily reprimanded by the other directors for neglecting their duties.

The figures for stout sales were seen as testimony to the success of the firm's efforts at improving its stout production. According to the acting chairman, the increase in the city trade in stout (up 761 barrels, while porter sales were down by 652) was 'very remarkable in face of the dullness of the labour market, and can only be accounted for by the merit of the company's manufacture'. Sales of stout also rose in the country, but these were offset by the drop in porter sales, which was attributed to the 'disastrous weather' in the late summer and autumn, which affected harvests. The price of malt rose by 1s 6d per barrel, but a reduction in the price of hops and other 'economies' reduced the impact.

Silver shield presented by the staff to the directors of the brewery in 1906.

Acquisitions

A major development occurred in February 1908 when the company acquired W. H. O'Sullivan and Sons mineral water manufacturers of Kilmallock, County Limerick, which had gone bankrupt (see highlight below). Within a year this concern had 'turned the corner', showed a profit and paid £128 into the coffers of James J. Murphy & Co. Ltd.

The year 1909 saw the company make further acquisitions. In August it purchased D. Donegan & Son's Maltings on nearby John Street for the sum of £4,056. This increased malting capacity considerably as this concern was bigger than the company's other maltings at the brewery itself, in Riverstown and on Devonshire

Street. The company saved £1,200 in the cost of malt in the following year as a direct result of the purchase. The other property acquired that year was the Bonding Stores on Leitrim Street, which were bought from the Cork Distillers' Co. In 1910-11 a swap of property with O'Connell and Co. of Little John Street 'squared' the oblong plot on which the brewery stood and consolidated the maltings. (Murphy's gave up some of their stores in Leitrim Street as their part of the deal.)

Cask Numbering Introduced

In 1908 a decision had been made to introduce a cask numbering system because of the increasing losses which the company was sustaining owing to the carelessness of traders

W. H. O'SULLIVAN AND SONS,
Kilmallock, County Limerick

The mineral water firm of W. H. O'Sullivan and Sons ('The Southern Mineral Waterworks') was founded in 1871 by William Henry O'Sullivan (1829-1887), who ran a hotel and car hire business in Kilmallock. He was a Fenian supporter and was nationalist MP for County Limerick from 1874 to 1885. The firm's mineral water bottles bore a distinctive yellow label,

illustrated with a drawing of the old Kilmallock Dominican priory and the legend 'Abbey Brand'. Business went well until 1908 when W. H. O'Sullivan and Sons got into serious financial difficulties and went into bankruptcy. In that year it was acquired by James J. Murphy & Co. Ltd, who continued the business under its old name.

The firm continued to manufacture mineral water, but now also became a major distributing and bottling centre for Murphy's Stout; this fact led the Kilmallock factory to be (inaccurately) referred to as 'The Brewery'. In

addition to stout and lemonade, W. H. O'Sullivan and Sons also bottled and distributed wines and spirits. They retailed a special, expensive brand of fifteen-year-old Jameson whiskey which was known as 'Kilmallock Red', on account of the colour of its label. The firm also traded in tea and corks for jars and bottles. The minerals manufactured at Kilmallock were lemonade, soda water, lemon soda, ginger ale and syphon soda. The factory used water from its own artesian well and the minerals had a high reputation.

Stout from Lady's Well Brewery was delivered by rail to the Kilmallock station, which was about half a mile from the factory, and a man was employed full-time collecting and delivering from the railway with a horse and float. During the time of the First World War O'Sullivan's were using about thirty horses and carts for deliveries, as well as a three ton petrol lorry, the first in the county, which was bought in 1914. The lorry did daily deliveries that could not be covered by horse. Its primary task was the delivery of large quantities of stout and minerals to the canteens in the British army camps at Ballyvonaire and Kilworth. The lorry, bearing the Murphy name, was an unusual sight trundling through the narrow roads and was considered a valuable advertisement for the company.

Kilmallock was among the first towns in Ireland to have its streets lit by electricity, and W. H. O'Sullivan's had a large role to play. In 1912 the firm supplied current from its newly installed electric generator to a number of pubs in the town, and extended this to providing some street lighting also. This lasted until 1923. In the late 1920s the firm supplied the workers' canteen at Ardnacrusha during the construction of the huge Shannon Hydroelectric Scheme.

The firm prospered over the next four decades, but in 1969 troubles at Murphy's led to the transfer of mineral bottling to the West Cork Bottling Co. in Bandon. In the mid-1970s O'Sullivans was reduced to a distribution depot, and in 1978, seventy years after Murphy's had begun its association with Kilmallock, business was moved from the town to Limerick city and the Kilmallock premises was sold off. The final link was broken in 1981 when the staff who had been transferred from Kilmallock were made redundant on the closing of the Limerick centre.

in returning casks. Guinness, who had been operating such a system for a considerable time, were contacted and 'very kindly' gave Murphy's 'every information on the subject'. The Guinness model was introduced on a limited and experimental basis in 1909, and its success in reducing loss of casks led to its extension to all districts in the following years.

Plant Improvements

There were a number of improvements to the plant in these years which led to more efficient production as well as an improved product. In 1910 a new vat house was completed while savings were made with the piping of steam from the boilers in the upper yard to the cask shed and cooling house engines, allowing the closure of the boilers there. Savings in labour were made by the installation of grain conveyors in the Devonshire Street grain store and the Lady's Well maltings.

A major outlay in this period was the erection of new aluminium vessels and the lining of old vessels with aluminium (fermentation vessels, tuns, etc.). A new 'Pure Air' plant was also erected and the laboratory was fully renovated, all of which improved the quality of the product 'enabling us to compete with our big opponent

[Guinness] on the point of merit'. The barley store and kiln on Leitrim Street was updated and connected to the brewery's maltings by pipes over the street. Barley was blown through the pipes to the higher floors of the malthouse, which led to savings in labour and carting.

Industrial Unrest

In 1907 a wave of trade union militancy began in Ireland. This movement was dubbed 'Larkinism' by the employers after its main driving force, James Larkin, and was characterised by the targeting of essential services like transport and the use of sympathetic strikes. The first serious strikes in Cork occurred in the summer of 1909, the year in which Larkin founded the Irish Transport and General Workers' Union (ITGWU). A dockers strike was supported by railway workers and carters and, as the strike spread, the employers organised themselves into the Cork Employers Federation and locked out anyone taking sympathetic action. Six thousand workers were eventually involved, directly or indirectly, and most trade and industry was seriously effected; there was trouble on the streets as strikers regularly clashed with the police. Murphy's had a wages dispute with its workers, but it was 'satisfactorily arranged'. The general dislocation of trade, however, cost the company in the region of £500, although they managed to keep most of their customers and agents supplied. The strike collapsed after five weeks and the hungry strikers returned to work. It was a significant victory for the employers of Cork and the ITGWU in the city disintegrated and did not re-establish itself there for another four years. 1911 saw a new wave of militancy in the wake of actions by the British Transport Workers

1908. Striking Cork dockers marching to meet trade union leader James Larkin. Note the James J. Murphy legend at the top of the public house (No. 1 Union Quay) in the background.

Federation. There was an all-out strike by the ITGWU in Dublin in July and in August-September members of the three main railway unions struck in Cork bringing services to and from the city to a standstill for a month. The strike caused enormous difficulties (the brewery incurred costs of £1,095) but also offered opportunities because Dublin was virtually cut off for the duration of the strike. This meant that Guinness could not supply its customers in the south and Murphy's moved to meet the deficit.

The steamers *Perseverence* and *Sard* were chartered and supplied Kenmare, Cahirciveen, Dingle and Tralee in County Kerry. Killarney and Kilorglin were supplied by rail to Macroom and from there by road. The steamer *Hope* ran east to Youghal and Dungarvan in County Waterford, and Lismore, also in Waterford, was supplied via Dungarvan. The Clyde Shipping Co. steamers supplied Limerick and inland agencies were supplied by road with horse and engine traction.

Meeting Demand

The extension of vat capacity which had been undertaken at the brewery allowed it to meet this sudden upsurge in demand, and matured stout in fine condition was ready for the market. 'The nett result', declared the chairman, 'is that we got the stout in, and we will make every effort to keep it there.' Despite the satisfaction of those new customers with Murphy's Stout and their promises to stay with it, only a small proportion of that trade was held. As the chairman pointed out, this emphasised 'the disadvantage we are at in fighting such a name as "Guinness" and the necessity of leaving nothing undone to produce an

article fully equal to, if not better than our big opponent'.

The large rise in output (up 3,000 barrels) which was necessary to meet the demand created by the railway strike, allied to the low cost of malt and coal, made 1911 a 'bumper year' with regard to profits. Nett profits rose from £29,986 in 1910 to £38,296. A coal strike in late 1911 and early 1912 saw the price of coal rise, while abnormally bad weather in late 1912 and early 1913 hit trade and led to a rise in the price of barley and malt. These factors led to a drop in profits over the next couple of years, until the war years brought the profits back up to the 1911-12 levels.

'Swam in Porter - Unique Occurrence in the City'

Further costs were incurred in 1913 when the No. 5 vat burst, an incident which attracted world-wide attention, with accounts carried in newspapers as far afield as New Zealand. About 23,000 gallons of drink, sweeping all before it, cascaded through the brewery and out onto Leitrim Street which, according to a newspaper account, became 'a river of porter'. A worker, who happened to be under the vat at the time of its collapse, had, according to the *Cork Constitution*, *a most exciting experience and in the onrush of porter he had to swim in it for about forty yards to save himself from asphixiation. As the liquor surged through the works the foreman played the firehose upon it, and diluted it to such a degree that it could not tempt people outside to indulge in it, and the unique incident had no regrettable results.*

As well as the costly loss of a considerable quantity of beer, the vat had to be replaced at a cost of £308 9s 7d.

Left: Brewery vats

HIGH JINKS AT THE JUBILEE
by Rex Archer

The sun shone in a cloudless sky all day long on Whit Monday in 1906. That was a matter of great satisfaction to Mr Richard Boland Tivy, General Manager of Murphy's Brewery, because he had taken upon himself the task of organising an outing of the entire workforce of the brewery to Killarney as part of the celebrations that were taking place to honour the Company's fifty years in business.

Mr Tivy was a short rotund man with a bald head, a high complexion and bloodshot eyes. Despite the best efforts of his barber, hair grew profusely from the end of his nostrils and out of his ears, giving him a fierce look which, coupled with a temper on a short fuse, made him a formidable man. He controlled the Brewery virtually single-handed because the easy-going Directors had discovered that this arrangement allowed them plenty of time for fox hunting and golf.

However Mr Tivy was all sweetness and light on this sunny Bank Holiday morning as he stood on the platform of Cork Railway Station supervising the arrival of his expectant workers. For, in his usual decisive fashion, he had hired a train to transport the 200 people involved. He smiled benignly as he noted that his guests were dressed in their 'Sunday Best', some of the more sporty members of the office staff were wearing straw boaters. The youngest worker present, in a cloth cap and short trousers, was thirteen year old Paddy Barrett, the office boy, who could recall the day vividly fifty years later, when he was Head Porter.

As the time for departure drew near, the Murphys and their ladies began to arrive and Mr Tivy's smile assumed a more deferential air as he escorted them to the first-class carriage reserved for the Family. The office clerks and the brewers, known as the Staff, were accommodated in the second-class carriages, while the rest, known as the Workers, had to be content to travel third-class. This undemocratic arrangement was accepted as quite normal by all, with the exception of one young man who protested, to no avail. He was treated with suspicion by most of his colleagues because he had declared openly that he was a socialist and he had failed, so far, to organise the workforce into a trade union.

The Murphy ladies were fashionably attired and drew ribald comments from some of the more junior clerks as Mr Tivy helped them to board the train. But not as much as that drawn by Mr Albert St. John Murphy when he arrived on the scene. Always a stylish dresser, he had settled for the outdoor look and cut a striking figure in russet-coloured tweed knickerbockers and jacket and the kind of large-brimmed hat favoured by Colonel 'Buffalo Bill' Cody for his touring Wild West Show.

Mr Tivy was consulting his watch prior to giving the signal to depart when Jim Creedon made an impressive entry. Jim was an office worker with theatrical ambitions and a lustful eye for the ladies. He was dressed in a straw boater, striped blazer and white trousers and looked as if he had just stepped down from a concert party stage. During the small cheer that his appearance drew from his colleagues, Mr Fitzjames Murphy was heard to remark, 'Doesn't Creedon look the complete bounder. All he's short is a ukulele.'

Everybody was aboard now so Mr Tivy joined the Family in their carriage, gave an imperious signal through the window, and they were off.

During the journey the Family were in an expansive mood, if not altogether exuberant, as they tolerated, with mild amusement, Tivy's efforts to charm the ladies. Things were a little more hectic in the second-class area where several highly-charged card games were soon under way and where Jim Creedon was entertaining some of the younger clerks with tales of his sexual prowess. He promised them that he would have it off with one or other of the younger Miss Murphys before the day was through. He expressed a preference for Miss Georgina Murphy, a statuesque blond beauty.

In the third-class carriages, however, it could be said that the golden jubilee celebrations had really commenced. From sad experience the 'Workers' had learned that Mr Tivy's idea of a good time and their's differed greatly and they had come prepared. Many had spent a few hours in their locals before setting forth and nearly everybody had brought a little something to keep body and soul together during the journey. Consequently, by the time the train passed through Mallow, it could be said that the party was in full swing.

When eventually the train reached Killarney there was a rush for Scott's Hotel where luncheon was served and many of those present noticed gratefully that there were several half-barrels of Murphy on tap around the dining-room.

Conversation and hilarity were suspended temporarily while the spring lamb and green peas were consumed and then Mr Tivy rose to say a few words. His face was a little more flushed than usual and his eyes had a mellow look, for the wine had been passed around freely at the top table. He welcomed everybody and outlined the programme for the rest of the day. It was then 3 p.m. and they were free, he told them, to spend the next few hours as they pleased, but they were to be back at the Hotel at 6 p.m. for high tea, after which there would be a musical evening. Then his eyes took on their customary hard-boiled look and he reminded them that they represented a highly respected firm and that they should avoid all excesses. He urged them to enjoy instead the scenic beauty which surrounded them. Then he and the Family left on jaunting cars for a trip around the lakes.

The records do not tell us how the rest of the guests spent the afternoon, but I think we can be certain that it wasn't looking at the scenery, because when they reassembled the sounds of merriment and high spirits rang around the dining-room as they tucked into the excellent mixed grill. The meal was enjoyed by all with the exception of Nedser O'Mahony who fell asleep at the table and was left undisturbed by his companions.

It is regrettable that the musical evening that followed the meal was not an unqualified success. The soloists had a problem in holding the interest of their audience, who tended to set up in opposition. At one time three different sing-songs were taking place simultaneously. However, after repeated calls for order, some attention was given to a performance by Tim O'Connell and Jim Creedon of the duet 'The Moon Hath Raised'. After that, chaos reigned again and Dan O'Shea's recitation of 'The Green Eye of the Little Yellow God' was largely unheard. It was at about this time that Nedser O'Mahony awoke from his slumbers and, rising to his feet, demanded a song from Mr Tivy. A tense silence descended on the room as everybody watched the Great Man. For a moment it looked as if a storm were about to erupt. His facial hair seemed to bristle and the hard-boiled look returned to his eyes, but then the general air of abandon took hold of him and with a smile he rose and gave a spirited rendering of 'Slattery's Mounted Foot'. His performance was the highlight of the evening and was received with thunderous applause. Nobody felt like following his act. Somebody called on Nedser to give them his well-known interpretation of 'The Light of Other Days', but Nedser had fallen asleep again, prompting Major James Murphy to remark that it looked as if the light had gone out.

It was now time to return to Cork and the weary revellers wound their way through the town to the Railway Station, where, after much confusion and head counting, the train pulled out from the platform.

So ended the Lady's Well Brewery Golden Jubilee excursion to Killarney, and a memorable day in the history of the firm.

Rex Archer worked at Lady's Well Brewery from 1939 to 1977. He began as an office clerk, later worked in sales and public relations, and served both as sales manager and as manager of the brewery's tied estate.

Lady's Well Brewery, 1906.

A First World War British Army recruiting poster.

6

Troubled Times

THE GREAT WAR, 1914-1918

We are fighting Germany, Austria and Drink; and as far as I can see the greatest of these three deadly foes is Drink.

Lloyd George, 1915

On 4 August 1914 the First World War, also known as the Great War, began. It lasted for over four years and was a watershed in the history of Europe and Ireland. On a smaller scale, it was also a turning point in the history of the brewery, marking as it did the beginning of a steady decline after over half a century of growth.

Joining Up

On the outbreak of war there was an immediate call on the men of Cork to enlist in the British army. There was no formal recruitment organisation until January 1915 and for the first five months recruitment was encouraged by the politicians, press, clergy and businessmen of the city. On 13 August James J. Murphy & Co. Ltd joined the other members of the Cork Employers Federation in promising that 'all constant employees volunteering to join any of His Majesty's forces for active service in compliance with the call for help by the Government will be facilitated and their places given back to them at the end of the war'. Eighteen of the brewery's workers joined up: fourteen in 1914, one each in the following two years, and two in 1917. The majority were in their late thirties and early

forties, so these were not young men seeking adventure and excitement. (There was one sixteen-year-old and four were in their twenties). All of those who enlisted (except one, who left without notice) were eligible for reappointment when and if they returned. Seven eventually came back to their old jobs; ten never returned, and some of them at least must have been among the thousands whose lives were wasted in the trenches of France and Belgium.

The Lady's Well workers were amongst approximately 6,000 others from the city (and around 200,000 in the country as a whole) who joined up during the war. Their reasons for doing so were varied. Some went for economic reasons,

others went for adventure, and many more answered the call of John Redmond, the Home Rule leader who believed a strong Irish contribution to the British war effort, supposedly

Right: The British Army recruiting office on Patrick's Street, Cork, during the First World War.

'Gassed', by John Singer Sargent.

in 'defence of small nations', would strengthen the case for Irish Home Rule at the war's end. A sarcastic jingle from the time went:

Full steam ahead, John Redmond said
that everything was well, chum;
Home Rule will come when we are dead
and buried out in Belgium.

As well as the seven of its own employees mentioned above, the brewery also took on five other former soldiers at the end of the war.

Donations and Subscriptions

In the first month of the conflict a National Relief Fund was established, and the Lord Mayor of Cork opened a subscription list for donations. James J. Murphy & Co. Ltd subscribed £500 and in the following month it was decided to start a voluntary weekly collection for the fund in the brewery. A collection bay was placed in the pay office where workers could give their donations, and it remained in place for the duration of the war. Sympathy with the plight of Belgium was one of the factors which encouraged many to enlist in the army, and Belgian refugees were welcomed in Cork. In August 1914 the board of directors gave £25 to the Belgian Refugees Fund as a first instalment. The Irish Red Cross was not established until the outbreak of the Second

World War, but the British-based organisation raised funds in Ireland throughout the First World War, laying stress on its non-partisan, international dimension. In October 1917 the board donated £100 to its fund. The company made more partisan contributions also; in 1917 it contributed money towards the purchase of ambulances for the 16th Irish Division fighting in France. The directors also contributed to the war effort by investing substantial sums in British government war loans, war bonds and Treasury Bills; the tens of thousands of pounds which the company invested in this way illustrated the strength of its capital reserves at this time.

In July 1919 the Irish National War Memorial Trust was set up to establish a permanent tribute to the Irishmen who had died in the war. James J. Murphy & Co. Ltd contributed £100, and the memorial was eventually opened in 1939 at Islandsbridge, County Dublin.

Dealings with the Military

On 6 August 1914, ten of the brewery's horses were requisitioned by the army who paid £60 each for them, and £5 for each set of harnesses. In January 1915 the firm agreed to allow the military to have use of their five ton Garrett steam engine, purchased the previous year, and

A wartime
advertisement for
the brewery,
stressing its role as
a supplier to British
Army canteens.

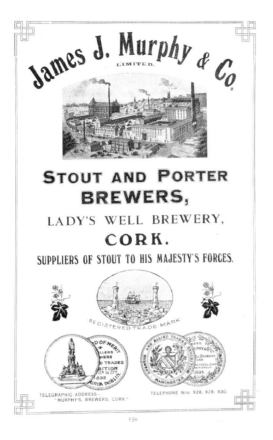

A wartime advertisement for the brewery, stressing its role as a supplier to British Army canteens.

granted on supplies to the army. There was stiff competition between the breweries for this trade. Representatives from James J. Murphy & Co. Ltd were constantly visiting barracks in the Cork and Munster area attempting to persuade them to take the firm's stout and porter. The chairman noted in his report for 1914 that ' . . . our canteen supply is increasing and our stout is giving the troops every satisfaction'.

The canteen at Bere Island was supplied by the brewery; a contract for Ballincollig barracks was secured in 1915, as was a portion of the supply to Fermoy. Other canteens, such as that at Kilworth, were supplied via W. H. O'Sullivan and Sons of Kilmallock, which was owned by Murphy's. In 1916 an agreement was reached to split the stout supply to Buttevant barracks with Beamish & Crawford (the ale was supplied by McArdle's); they had previously been supplied by the British brewery Worthingtons.

James J. Murphy & Co. Ltd touted for business in places as far away as Aldershot in England (where Beamish & Crawford had part of the supply), while in 1916 it received requests, which it could not meet due to restrictions, to supply stout to Irish soldiers in Flanders and in France. Often, the opinion of the colonel in charge was crucial in determining the brands which would be supplied. In 1915 the supply of Murphy's Stout to the Templemore canteen in County Tipperary was stopped by the colonel there who ordered Guinness instead, although there had been no complaints from the men about the Murphy's. Colonel Creagh of the 3rd Munsters at Tralee told Murphy's early in the war that although he personally favoured the Cork brewery's XX Stout, if he ordered it, the men would go into the town to drink Guinness.

its driver on request. The company also leased stores to the military; their Pine Street store was leased for £7 10s per month from 1916; later the army also rented the stores at Leitrim Street and Devonshire Street at a cost of £15 per month. They were returned towards the end of the war with 'everything in order'.

Army Canteens

After Dublin and the Curragh in County Kildare, the Cork area had the largest concentration of soldiers in the country; the railway station and port also made it an important pass-through area. The army canteen trade was very important, both because of the numbers of thirsty consumers it provided and because exemptions to the restrictions on output were

A major coup was achieved in 1916 when the firm finally managed to break the Beamish & Crawford monopoly on supply to the Cork Barracks. In March of that year Murphy's was finally granted joint supply with its Cork competitor 'after many years of trying to get in' and a period of intensive lobbying during which it was argued that the Beamish & Crawford monopoly was unfair and that the supply to the city barracks should be shared between the two local breweries. On the 14th of that month the first consignment of Murphy's Stout was delivered to the canteen on Barrack Street.

Following the foundation of the Irish Free State in December 1922, the army canteen representative called to the brewery on behalf of his new employers, the Irish government. The board noted that 'we should do all we can to get in', and in the following months supply was secured to barracks at Fermoy, Cahir, Clonmel, Kilmacthomas, Waterford city, Wexford and Kilkenny.

Impact of the War on the Brewing Industry

As the war progressed the British government extended state control over most of the economy in an effort to maximise the war effort. All industries were affected, but brewing was particularly hard hit. Lloyd George (Chancellor of the Exchequer at the outbreak of war, Minister for Munitions from May 1915 and British prime minister from December 1916) was a temperance supporter and was hostile to the drinks industry. He constantly pointed to the negative effect of excessive drinking on war production through drunkenness and absenteeism, declaring in 1915 that 'Drink is doing us more damage in the war

than all the German submarines put together.' Although the south of Ireland had little direct role in war production (it was limited to a number of small munitions factories, the munitions box trade and shipbuilding), the drinks industry there suffered the same restrictions as in the rest of the United Kingdom. In 1916 a Food Controller was appointed as the German submarine campaign was having an impact on food supplies and from 1917 government policies were directed increasingly towards maximising food supply which had important implications for the brewing industry, as we shall see.

Under the Defence of the Realm Act there were draconian reductions in opening hours. The military, and later the civil authorities were given the power to close pubs and/or restrict opening hours. In the first weeks of the war a number of Murphy's tied houses in country areas such as Crosshaven, Rafeen and Shanbally were closed down temporarily by the military for supplying soldiers against their orders.

Government policy in the early years of the war was concerned mainly with reducing consumption of alcohol among soldiers and workers, through restricting licences and opening hours, and also by price rises, which involved huge rises in duties (which had the added advantage of increasing government revenue). Drink had always been a favourite target for government taxation. The increase in the tax burden between 1914 and 1920 in real terms (allowing for wartime inflation) was of the order of 430 per cent. By the end of the war duty accounted for five-eigths of the price of a pint. The duties were not lifted at the war's end and tax had become the major element in determining the price of drink (as it remains to this day). Restricted opening hours also remained in place after the ending of hostilities.

By 1917 the full impact of the war was felt by the industry. There were widespread lay-offs in the breweries and ancilliary industries such as pubs and bottling firms. By May of that year seventy-two workers at Lady's Well had been laid off as a result of the wartime restrictions, approximately one-third of the workforce of 1914.

THE BREWERY IN THE WAR YEARS: TRADE AND PROFITS

1914

When the war broke out in August 1914 the brewery's trade was on the increase. It had been slack in the first half of the year due to wet weather and a cattle embargo resulting from an outbreak of foot and mouth disease. Improved weather in the summer, the 'excellence' of Murphy's stout and porter which was continuing to gain public favour, and the mobilisation of the army all led to a sharp upswing in trade in the second half of the year. The upswing was halted, however, by a price rise in the budget of November which imposed an increase in duty of 17s 3d on a barrel and a halfpenny on a pint of beer. This brought the price of a pint of stout up to 3d. The board followed Guinness in upping the price of a gallon of porter by 7d and of stout by 8d. The vintners requested the brewers to absorb the price rises but they refused. A number of the company's customers continued to sell at the old price and had to be pulled into line. Nett profits for the year amounted to £23,191 on sales of £286,292.

David Lloyd George, Chancellor of the Exchequer for the first two years of the war and British Prime Minister from December 1916.

1915

Trade continued to shrink in 1915 due to increased duties, however nett profits rose to £36,174. This rise was the result of a further halfpenny increase in the sale price of the pint imposed by the Chancellor of the Exchequer, and an overall drop in costs. Although barley prices reached their highest level ever, the cost of hops was down; a contract for coal at a very good price was secured, and a surplus was maintained in line with a policy to build up reserves 'to be a source of strength to us should a further pinch

come'. Improved methods in the engineering department led to a reduction in coal and water consumption, while outlay on the plant was down due to the postponement of the aluminium lining of the old wooden vessels due to wartime shortages. Other economies which had been put in place in the previous year included the installation of a pneumatic tube for the transfer of barley from the Leitrim Street store to the maltings at the brewery. The use of the new steam engine speeded up transport between the brewery and another of its maltings at Riverstown, outside the city.

1916

By 1916 the war was beginning to impact more heavily on the brewing trade and it was, according to the chairman, a year of 'much anxiety for all brewers'. As German submarines began to take their toll on British merchant shipping, the government responded by restricting brewing output by legislation in August and December, with the aim of reducing import requirements as well as encouraging sobriety. The new restrictions caused many difficulties for James J. Murphy & Co. Ltd as it tried to keep its agents and individual traders supplied while remaining within the legal limits. Demand was high as a result of increased spending power in rural areas due to the increased value of agricultural produce. Demand was further increased in April following the Easter Rising (see p. 85), or 'the rebellious rising' as it was described in the minutes of the company board meeting. The disruption resulting from the rising led to a temporary halting of supplies of Guinness from Dublin and consequent pressure from town and country pubs to be supplied with Murphy's. However, the restrictions and the level of available stock meant that the brewery could only supply its own trade and was unable to take advantage of the situation.

Among the crops which increased in value in 1916 was barley, which of course impacted on the brewery. It opened at 23s per barrel and rose to 36s due to the entry of British maltsters to the market because of shortages there and also the late entry of Guinness. Coal prices were also up but the cost of hops was minimised due to judicious buying. Plant maintenance costs also rose as did the wages bill due to the granting of war bonuses to workers to offset huge cost of living increases. Despite increased costs and output restrictions, profits were slightly up at £39,335. This was mainly due to further increases in the price of stout and porter in June, allied to lower carriage and commission figures due to the curtailment of trade.

While exports of stout and porter had been in decline, the war accelerated this process. In April the firm closed down its agencies in Manchester and Newport because of increased freight charges and reduced trade due to the output restrictions. (The Newport agency was reopened in June on the request of the agent, at an increase of 5 per cent on prices.)

Despite the maintenance of profit levels the chairman, Francis Murphy, saw the disadvantages of the situation in the longer term. In his annual report to the shareholders for the year of 1916, he declared:

We are at war and only too happy to help to end it in any way the Government would call on us to do, but still we cannot help regretting that our trade curtailment occurred at this particular time just as we were beginning to reap the benefit of the large expenditure made in connection with the lining of our old vessels with aluminium and the erection of new vessels in the same material by which the keeping qualities of our stouts and porter had been greatly improved. In fact the difficulty of holding the market against Guinness was every day growing less. As an example of this, our Kilmallock factory which is practically in the midst

of a Guinness district, and where we were compelled to sell Guinness with ours, has not bottled Guinness for the past ten years and with our stout only has not alone held the trade but increased it - a very fair test of quality.

1917

The chairman declared 1917 another 'very anxious and troublesome year in the Brewing trade'. In March, as the supply situation worsened, the Food Controller introduced an order limiting brewing output to a mere 28 per cent of the pre-war level, or a third of that of 1915-16. The new target was accompanied by restrictions on malting and the requisitioning of barely in line with government policy of diverting cereals away from brewing and distilling and towards direct human consu-mption. The full reduction in output was never made as a result of lobbying by the brewers, the

earmarking of additional output for military canteens and the realisation that the shortage of beer had been a major factor in sparking industrial unrest in the summer of 1917. However, the reduction led to the laying off (bet-ween March and May) of forty-six workers at Lady's Well, about 25 per cent of the workforce at the time. The company's maltings (at the brewery, in John Street, Devonshire Street and

Riverstown) were closed down on 10 February as barley steeping was stopped by the Food Controller and the stocks of barley were taken over by the Ministry of Food. The thirty-three workers involved in malting were all laid off. The brewery was allowed to keep malt, but not enough to carry it through to the new season, forcing it to buy from those with a surplus (from a clearing house). A portion of the firm's barley was sold to local millers and the rest was sent to England. Steeping began again in September.

Further reduction in the use of cereals was achieved by the enforced lowering of the strength, or gravity, of beers. The government initially ordered that all beer be brewed at a gravity of 1036 degrees. This was regarded as 'manifestly unfair' by the Irish brewers, whose beer, on average, had a higher gravity than that of their English counterparts. The Irish average was 1066 as against an English average of 1050. The order would thus have meant a thirty degree drop in strength for Irish beer as against only fourteen for the English. There was strong opposition from the Irish brewing trade, and several deputations, of which Charles Eustace Murphy was an active member, met with the Food Controller on the issue. They pointed to the unfairness involved in the extra weakening of the Irish product and also to the fact that brewing was more central to Irish agriculture. Their lobbying led to a compromise, and a rise in permitted gravity to 1042. In the following year of 1918 the gravity was reduced to 1030, but Ireland was exempted and gravity there was fixed at 1045. In August 1919 output restrictions were lifted but an average permitted gravity remained: 1044 for Britain and 1051 for Ireland. Restrictions on gravity were lifted in 1921, but there was no attempt to restore the old gravities because increases in duty, which was linked to the gravity, would have meant increases in prices and a consequent reduction in sales.

In 1917 the question of nationalisation of the brewing industry (as well as distilling and the retail drinks industry) was considered by the government. Committees were established to consider the financial implications, and Charles Eustace Murphy joined the other Irish brewers in making submissions on the practicalities of state purchase to the Irish committee. He suggested that 'if we received 20 years purchase based on our income tax we would be prepared to accept it'. This suggestion was regarded as the most practical by the committee, but the national-isation idea was soon abandoned by the government. Either the scheme would have been too expensive and inconvenient, or perhaps the threat of compulsory state purchase was being used as a stick to beat the brewers into accepting more controls; these were duly imposed, with the further reduction in gravities in 1918.

By April the price of a pint of stout stood at 5d and in that month an agreement was made with Beamish & Crawford not to supply any customers who sold below that price. (At the war's end the price of a pint of porter stood at 8d and a pint of stout was 9d.) In September a further agreement was reached with Beamish & Crawford that neither brewery would supply the agents or customers of the other.

Wages, general charges and the costs of the basic raw materials of barley, hops and coal were all up in 1917. A coal famine was feared in Cork in the upcoming winter due to the number of cargo steamers taken over by the government. The brewery was able to hold five months stock in reserve in case of such an eventuality. Despite all of this, nett profits, at £38,396, were only slightly down on those of 1916. There were a number of reasons for this: a price rise by Guinness in August was again followed by all brewers (so that the old 2d pint was now almost 6d), yet demand remained high, especially in rural areas where farmers were doing well from the war; the restrictions on output meant an end to local competition (note the agreements with Beamish & Crawford mentioned above), which also helped to keep prices up and 'make business more lucrative'; and the enforced weakening of beer reduced unit costs. Thus, despite all the restrictions and irksome controls, the chairman was able to report that, for the year of 1917, the 'final figures show the Brewery to be in a very strong financial position indeed . . .'

1918

1918, the last year of the war (which ended in November in victory for Britain and its allies), was another one of 'restriction and strain'. March saw the imposition of a further reduction in output as well as fresh controls on malting, in order to release barley for bread. The Murphy's barley surplus was again taken over by the Food Controller and disposed of 'at his own sweet will' (in the words of the chairman). There was the expected shortage of coal and the Coal Controller ordered the use of turf in order to conserve coal stocks. Further savings on coal were achieved by running certain machinery on electricity, and the electrification of the plant, with the reduction to a minimum of steam, was seriously considered. Other modernisation measures which were considered included the replacement of the absorption cooling plant with a compression one which would have been less expensive and more efficient. Improvements which were undertaken included the installation of new malt mills which increased malt extracts and the resurfacing of

The middle yard at Lady's Well Brewery. The yards were resurfaced with asphalt in 1918.

the cellar floors and the three yards with asphalt. The yards had always been a source of trouble, as they became too muddy in winter and too dusty in summer. Despite the high cost, there was satisfaction that the new surfaces would result in improved cleanliness and savings in upkeep.

A further increase in duty from 25s to 50s per standard barrel in July led to a further price increase to the trade. As on previous occasions, the increases were passed on to the public and the trade gained, with the result that, according to the chairman, 'many accounts in our ledgers which we did not expect to be cleared for years to come have disappeared and credit balances created in many instances in their stead'. The company's own nett profits for the year were up by £3,392.

This reflected the general situation with regard to profits during the war years. In general, the impact of government controls (reduced gravities, restricted output and competition, price rises, etc.) resulted in the protection and, in many cases, the enhancement of profits for the industry and the trade. In the longer term, however, James J. Murphy & Co. Ltd's steady advance at the expense of its

competitors had been halted. There had been a shift to lower consumption levels, with higher prices and reduced opening hours, while extra stout was now at a lower gravity than porter was at the beginning of the war. Despite improvements to the plant and its product in the years ahead, the long term decline of the company had begun.

WORKERS, TRADE UNIONS AND STRIKES, 1916-23

They have taken untold millions that they never toiled to earn,
But without our brains and muscle not a single wheel can turn,
We can break their haughty power; gain our freedom when we learn
That the union makes us strong.

(Lines from the trade union song 'Solidarity Forever', 1915)

The Irish labour movement was in a poor state on the eve of the Great War, following the defeat of the Dublin general strike and the great lock-out of 1913. The latter part of the war, however, saw a vast improvement in its fortunes. While farmers and employers prospered in the war years, workers suffered as wage rates failed to keep pace with spiralling inflation, particularly the huge price rises in food. By the end of 1916 retail food prices were 84 per cent above their July 1914 level, while the best paid workers were earning no more than 20 per cent above their pre-war wages. Throughout 1915-16, employers, including James J. Murphy & Co. Ltd, successfully resisted demands from their workers for wage increases. They did, however, begin to pay a 'war bonus', which they regarded as an exceptional and temporary measure designed to meet the extraordinary demands of wartime. (As inflation continued, however, these bonuses came to be incorporated into basic wage rates.)

As the war progressed and employers showed no intention of sharing any of their 'spoils of war' with their employees, workers

began to organise and flex their industrial muscles in pursuit of their demands. Trade unionism flourished, accompanied by an upsurge in strikes and demands for wage increases, reduced working hours and paid holidays.

War Bonus

In May 1915 demands from the workers at Lady's Well for increased pay to meet the increased cost of living led to the granting of a war bonus of one shilling a week. In May 1916 this was increased to 2s and in November was doubled to 4s. In April 1917 it was decided, with the agreement of the workers, to close the 'tap', the free beer allowance to which all brewery workers were entitled, and pay them an extra 2s per week

instead. By November 1917 the total bonus amounted to 10s per week.

In February 1916 the firm's malt house men served the company with strike notice in pursuit of their demand for double pay for Sundays. They were in a weak position, however, because their action was opposed by the Cork Brewery Workmen's Society which represented the brewery labourers. The company sacked all the strikers, confident that they would have 'very little trouble in getting men to replace them'. A week later seventeen new men were taken on at the malt house. In the following years, however, increased workers' organisation and solidarity transformed the situation.

The ITGWU

Wages in all sectors of the brewery continued to rise over the following three years in response to demands from labourers and tradesmen. The tradesmen had long been organised in the old trades societies such as the Coopers' Society and the Carpenters and Joiners' Society, and they won substantial increases throughout 1917-18. They were now joined by the labourers who were organised, along with the Beamish & Crawford workers, in the Cork Brewery Workmen's Society, which in 1920 was absorbed by the rapidly expanding Irish Transport and General Workers' Union (ITGWU). The malsters and other employees of the company, including those in Kilmallock, also joined the ITGWU.

Labour unrest in the brewery grew throughout 1919. Wages were increased in February and May by 5s each time in response to the increasingly strong workers' demands, although the demand for a reduction in the working week from fifty to forty-seven hours was

Left: The brewery's boilermen.

£1 = 20s
1s = 12d

82

successfully resisted by the company. The labourers' pre-war wages of 20s per week now stood at 50s (£2 10s). In November a further £1 per week and a week's paid annual holiday were demanded, and they again sought a reduction (in line with that gained by a number of the trades) of the working week from fifty hours to forty-seven. The company directors, along with those at Beamish & Crawford, argued that the workers were exaggerating the cost of living and that they were getting among the highest labourers' wages in the city. The breweries' refusal to accede to the union's demands led to strike notice being served on 30 January 1920, and on 11 February 300 workers in the two city breweries began their strike.

1920 Strike

The breweries held out for five weeks, during which time output was seriously effected. A longer-term consequence of the strike was that, in the words of the chairman, '. . . it opened the way for Guinness to get into many of our houses and out of which we are finding it very hard to oust him'. The foothold which Guinness gained in the city's trade during this time was never subsequently relinquished.

After five weeks a compromise was reached between the strikers and the breweries; the latter agreed to a 12s 6d per week pay increase, a reduction of two and a half hours in the working week, and an agreement in principle on paid holidays. The strike ended on 15 March and the strikers returned to work on the following day. The success of the strike was due in no small way to the solidarity shown by other brewery employees. The malsters refused to steep any more barley once the strike began, while the Coopers' Society, whose members were traditionally hostile to unskilled workers, contributed generously to the strike fund and refused to do labourers' work. All brewery workers were granted the same concessions as the labourers, except for the coopers and other tradesmen, who nevertheless continued to win wage increases, conces-sions in hours and productivity bonuses. The coopers reached their highest level of earnings in May 1920 when all the trades won increases, while a strike by carpenters in September won them a further increase of £1 per week and a three hour reduction in their working week. On the 20th of that month all brewery workers (excluding the tradesmen) received a further pay increase of 7s 6d per week. In the following month the engineers' wages were increased by 7s 6d per week to £4, while the company reached an agreement with the ITGWU to grant an annual week's paid holiday to men employed for at least twelve months.

Further Gains for Workers

In June of 1921 the coopers, mechanics, painters, fitters, carpenters and outside carpenters sought and won the one week's annual paid holiday granted to the labourers. (They were asked by Charles Eustace Murphy during the negotiations to request and consume Murphy's and also to 'talk it up', as this would ultimately be to the benefit of both workers and employers.) In the following month there was a dispute between the company and the ITGWU with regard to holidays. The board was insisting that no holidays could be taken during the brewery's busiest period between July and September. The men, however, wanted summer holidays as was the norm in other Cork firms. The union urged the directors to accede to their demands or 'serious trouble was likely to ensue'. Fearful of a repeat of the damaging strike of the previous year, the board offered a compromise whereby holidays could begin on 8 August in 1921, and from 1922 they would be between March and June inclusive and again from the end of September. The offer was accepted by the men.

The overall effect of this period of militant trade unionism was a major improvement in the working conditions, standard of living and quality of life for the brewery workers, particularly the unskilled. They now worked shorter hours, enjoyed a paid annual holiday, while, in real terms, labourers wages were up by 60 per cent on their pre-war value. Wage rates of unskilled workers, which before the war had

stood at about half that of their skilled counterparts, had by 1921 risen to approximately 70 per cent of those of the tradesmen.

Syndicalism

Besides the strikes at Lady's Well itself, the general upsurge in industrial unrest in Ireland between 1917 and 1923 (known as Ireland's syndicalist years) also impacted on the brewery. In 1918, for example, the labourers at the company's Kilmallock factory were granted a 3s wage increase because of the success of a general strike in nearby Charleville in winning a similar pay rise for workers there. In 1919 plans for extending the mashing plant at Lady's Well were disrupted due to a moulders' strike which paralysed the engineering trade for many months. In January 1920 the firm's lorries were warned off the streets by striking lorry drivers, while in January-February 1922 a strike on all the railway lines in the Cork region (for 'twenty-four red hours' on 11-12 February the workers ran their own timetable) seriously disrupted deliveries to the county and general Munster area. During a strike at Beamish & Crawford's factory in Bandon in the same month, James J. Murphy & Co. Ltd moved quickly to supply Beamish customers in pursuit of the all important aim of 'keeping Guinness out'. Both Cork breweries received a boost in this regard in the following year when trade unions in the city organised a campaign against the Dublin firm.

Workers' Campaign Against Guinness

In August 1923 the Coopers' Society called a meeting of the different trades in the brewery to organise a labour campaign 'against the consumption of Guinness as being against labour and so much money going to Dublin against the interest of the city [Cork]'. A meeting was subsequently held with the brewery labourers (affiliated to the ITGWU) and clerical staff (non-union) 'to confer as to the best method of promoting the sale of local stouts as against Guinness'. It was estimated that, between wages and salaries, Guinness spent only £280 per week in Cork city, and the workers believed that their future employment depended upon supporting the local breweries. In September the transport workers stopped delivering Guinness to the pubs of the city and suburbs, and James J. Murphy & Co. Ltd was happy to supply any orders for bottled stout in bulk which arose from the shortfall. The board made clear to the ITGWU in the brewery that it would countenance nothing in the way of a boycott or coercive measures. It told its workers that it was perfectly legitimate to demand support for local brewers 'so long as they produced an article to compete with Guinness. The fight must be a clean one. We would support them if they fought on those lines.'

THE WAR OF INDEPENDENCE AND CIVIL WAR, 1919-23

Now never marry a soldier,
a sailor or a marine,
But keep your eye on the Sinn Féin boy
with his yellow, white and green.

('Salonika')

Right: A group of Black and Tans at Cork's Union Quay, 1920.

By the time the First World War ended in November 1918, the political situation in Ireland had been transformed. On Easter Monday 1916 a group of Irish nationalists, acting on the old Fenian belief that 'England's difficulty is Ireland's opportunity', staged an armed rebellion in Dublin and proclaimed an Irish Republic. The rebellion was easily crushed militarily, but the subsequent execution of fifteen of its leaders, the imposition of martial law and the arrest of thousands of nationalists led to widespread resentment. The threat of conscription, which had been introduced in England in early 1916, hung over the country and there was widespread opposition to it. When the British finally extended it to Ireland in April 1918, there was such intense opposition, including a one-day general strike, that the measure was abandoned. The new mood in the country saw popular support swing away from the constitutional nationalist Irish Party of John Redmond, which sought home rule for Ireland and supported Britain in the war, and towards the rejuvenated Sinn Féin, the separatist, Republican party which supported the 1916 rebels and opposed conscription.

War of Independence, 1919-21

In the general election of December 1918 Sinn Féin won a majority in Ireland, though not in the area that would become Northern Ireland, where Unionists, who supported the link with Britain, outnumbered nationalists. Sinn Féin refused to attend the British parliament, and constituted

itself as Dáil Éireann, the parliament of Ireland, on 21 January 1919. On the same day a group of Irish Volunteers (the organisation which had been predominant in the 1916 rising) ambushed a police convoy in County Tipperary and fired the first shots in what would become a two-and-a-half year guerrilla war waged by the Volunteers, who became known as the Irish Republican Army (IRA). This conflict (known as the War of Independence, the Troubles or the Anglo-Irish War) saw the IRA stage ambushes, raids on police barracks and assassinations. In response, the British reinforced the police with two new forces, the Auxiliaries and the notorious 'Black and Tans', made up of demobbed British soldiers who had served in the Great War. Their activities inflicted terror on the population and increased support for the rebels. Curfews were imposed, houses were raided, markets and fairs were stopped, many co-operative creameries were burned or closed by the military, and towns were looted and also burned. The Munster region was particularly affected. Many people died including the Lord Mayor of Cork, Tomás MacCurtain who was shot, and his successor as Lord Mayor, Terence MacSwiney, who died after a hunger strike in Brixton prison in England. McSwiney, as mentioned in Chapter 1, was married to Muriel Frances Murphy, a cousin of the brewery founders.

Stout Supplants Porter

The 'troubles' did not become serious enough to impact on the brewery until 1920. In 1919, following the ending of the First World War, there was a brief economic boom associated with the release of 'pent-up' consumer demand and the easing of restrictions on trade. The sudden lifting of the restrictions on output in July caught brewers unprepared, but James J. Murphy & Co. Ltd managed to meet the large increase in demand in town and country. The change in the nature of that demand (the increasing preference for stout over porter) which had begun before the war was now becoming even more evident. The shift towards the stronger of the black beers was attributed by the chairman to 'the increased circulation of money and the consequent tendency on the part of the public to buy the best article'. There was also the fact that with reductions in gravities, porter was but a shadow of its former self. This trend, which was stronger in the city trade, continued in the following years. By 1921 the chairman reported that 'Porter is now practically dead in the South of Ireland'. He believed that the modernisation of the brewing plant and machinery which had been carried out over the previous years placed the company 'in a position to meet this change, especially on the point of "merit", for in these days of keen competition it is chiefly merit that counts', and that had they not paid close attention to the production of stout and maintained its high quality, 'we would have found ourselves in a very dangerous position today'. Murphy's porter was supplied to the city pubs for the last time in 1926; it continued to be consumed in ever decreasing quantities in rural areas until 1943, when it was finally taken off the market.

The Troubles Begin to Impact on the Brewery

Despite increases in beer duty, wages and other costs, the balance sheet for 1919 was still satisfactory, principally due to healthy trading figures. The figures for 1920, however, showed a marked disimprovement. The five week strike in the brewery (see p. 83) in January and February had seen the year begin on a bad footing for the company, and as 1920 progressed, the prevailing unrest in the country was beginning to seriously interfere with trade. There was disruption of traffic, pubs were being closed early, fairs in country towns were stopped, and country people were being prevented from coming to towns, including Cork city, which reduced the amount of money in circulation. The ending of the post-war boom towards the end of 1920 added to the gloom.

The Burning of Cork

In the second half of 1920 the British forces burnt and partially destroyed a number of towns

Patrick's Street, Cork after the burning of the city by British forces, December 1920. Four of the brewery's tied houses were destroyed in the fires.

in the brewery's catchment area (including Mallow), crippling them commercially. The culmination of this period of destruction occurred on 11-12 December when the centre of Cork city was extensively damaged by fire. An estimated £3m worth of goods and property were destroyed, including four of the company's tied

houses: two in George's Street (now Oliver Plunkett Street), one in Cook Street and one in Maylor Street. The company was eventually compensated for its losses by the British government, and the four destroyed premises were sold off.

Improvements to the Plant

Despite the prevailing unrest and disruption, the company continued to modernise and upgrade the brewery throughout 1920. The old No. 2 mash tun was replaced and work began on a new house and plant for the roasting of malt. New workshops in the upper yard were completed and all the mechanical departments, which had hitherto been scattered throughout the brewery, were now housed under the same roof, which meant savings in time and money. A further development involved an agreement with the Cork Electric Lighting Company for it to supplement the brewery's own electricity supply, which led to an increase in the use of electrical motor power. (The offices were lit by the Electricity company since late 1916.)

Transport: the Advent of the Petrol Lorry

Another major development in this period was the change in the nature of the forms of transport used by the brewery. Up to the beginning of the Great War, horses were used for most transport purposes while the railways were utilised for longer journeys out of the city. In 1914 a five ton Garret steam engine was bought for railway delivery work in the summer and to run barley and malt between Lady's Well and the maltings at Riverstown, outside the city. In the same year, a three ton motor lorry was purchased for the

and expensive and the use of the lorries speeded up deliveries and led to a reduction in transport costs. The brewery continued to maintain its stables and use horses for deliveries, especially in the city, but the chairman acknowledged that 'undoubtedly the "motor" will supercede the old horse traction'.

In 1920 arrangements were made for installing storage tanks and pumps for petrol at Lady's Well. A three-and-a-half ton Fiat lorry was bought for Kilmallock and in December the old three tonner from Kilmallock was moved to Cork and replaced by two one ton Fords. Seven old horse drawn drays were sold off during the year and (in a symbolic illustration of changing times) when the brewery's wheelwright died in November, the board's minutes noted that 'This position will not again be filled.'

Kilmallock branch and in August a similar vehicle was ordered for Cork from Thompson's in Dublin. Only two ton lorries were available, however, because that firm's stock was taken over by the government for war purposes, and the order was cancelled. The brewery had to wait until the war's end to purchase its first lorries. The Kilmallock lorry, however, was succesfully utilised during the war for daily deliveries that could not be covered by horse, 'and as an advertisement was of much value'. A plan to transfer it to Cork and replace it with a two ton vehicle was not proceeded with.

In May 1919 a decision was taken to buy the first four or five ton lorry which became available. At the end of that month a four ton Leyland was purchased for £1,227 9s. The platform was enlarged and the Murphy name was put on the canopy. A couple of days later a two ton 'Commer' lorry (a W&G or Commercial Car) was bought for £800 and at the end of June a five ton 'Karrier' was purchased. Drivers were appointed for the lorries, and in September a fourth driver was taken on as a standby for the lorries and as a chauffeur for the new four-seater Ford car which was bought for the use of 'the office'. The old steam engine was disposed of; it was still in good condition but, compared to petrol motor traction, it was far too slow and cumbersome. Hired horse carters were also slow

Bottling at the Brewery Begins

Hostilities continued in Ireland throughout the first half of 1921 and impacted on trade. Roads were cut up by trenches, bridges were made impassable and railways were closed down for periods. The conflict had by now entered a stalemate and pressure from British, American and world public opinion led to a truce in July and the beginning of negotiations on a settlement. (In the meantime, in June 1921, the parliament of the six counties of Northern Ireland had been opened and the partition of Ireland was established.)

In the early part of the year the company took the landmark decision to begin bottling its own stout at the brewery. Prior to this stout was bottled by local bottling companies and by the pubs themselves. The principal reason for this initiative was that many publicans were not being very careful in bottling Murphy's stout and were not too concerned about the purity of the product which they sold to the public. The problems with quality and consistency were arising at the very time when consumption of bottled stout was increasing.

Bottling at the brewery began in June using hand machines, and later the old ice house was converted into a bottling plant. A foreman and four 'boys' were installed to run the operation, new machinery was bought, and new labels bearing the legend 'Bottled at the Brewery' were designed. The brewery was now in a position to monitor and guarantee the quality and consistency of its bottled product, and could 'put our stout properly bottled before the public'. The improvement was noticed immediately by

The brewery's first bottling plant which began operations in 1921.

customers and a good trade was established. The bottling department proved to be a good source of revenue (although it was refused an off-licence in September 1922) and the improved product helped the draught trade also. Publicans continued to bottle stout themselves, but the company kept up pressure on them to take that bottled at the brewery on the basis that it would be beneficial to both parties.

Improvements to both the bottled and draught product (the latter resulting from plant improvements) saw the chairman report in 1921 that the company's travellers were reporting that 'the public are finding out there is another stout equally as good as Guinness - it is a strong point gained and the improved conditions in the country and the greater circulation of money in the coming year should bring us a substantial improvement in trade'.

Civil War, 1922-23

The optimism about 'improved conditions' was short-lived, however, and 1922 saw the recommencement of hostilities, this time in the form of civil war. This resulted in the year of 1922 being, according to the chairman, 'one of the most anxious and strenuous that the brewery has yet experienced'.

The terms of the Anglo-Irish Treaty, signed in December 1921, resulted in a split in the Irish independence movement. While the majority, led by Michael Collins, believed the Treaty was the best deal achievable and offered 'the freedom to achieve freedom', a large minority led by Éamon de Valera refused to accept an agreement which involved an oath of allegiance to the British king. British troops and administrators withdrew from the twenty-six counties and control was handed over to a Provisional Government and National Army made up of that portion of Sinn Féin and the IRA which accepted the Treaty. Civil War broke out in June 1922, and a bitter ten-month struggle between the National Army and the 'Irregulars' or Republicans ensued.

By the end of July the Republicans had been overcome in most areas of the country, but held out in the so-called 'Munster Republic', an area south of a line running from Limerick to Waterford, which was also the stronghold of James J. Murphy & Co. Ltd's trade. Ambushes, the bombing of bridges, and general unrest created serious difficulties for the brewery. Disruption to railway traffic (both as a result of the Troubles and also due to strikes) meant increased transport costs, with the hiring of carters and lorries at exorbitant prices. The firm's lorries were commandeered by both sides and a number of consignments were hijacked, while roads were frequently closed by Republican forces. In August, the National Army captured Cork city and the Republicans evacuated and moved west.

Brewery Workers in the IRA

In July and August of 1922 eight men and boys from the cellar, vats, malt gang and the wash, as well as an electrician and a lorry driver, left the brewery to join the Republican forces. Following the evacuation of the city they applied to come back to their jobs, but the board initially decided not to reinstate them. That decision was subsequently rescinded when the directors accepted that the men had apparently left 'more or less under compulsion from the IRA'. (Back in March 1867, on the morning following the abortive Fenian rising, scarcely half the brewery's employees turned up for work having left the city the previous night to launch the rising in rural areas.)

Chartered Steamers

In August 1922 the company took two important measures in response to the transport difficulties which it was facing. Initially, to supply the coastal trade, it began the expensive policy of hiring motor driven fishing boats. It was then decided to charter a steamer from Dublin, the *Cheviot*, to deliver supplies and collect empties along the coast. It usually went as far as Tralee, and occasionally to Limerick and even as far as Galway. The cost of chartering and running the boat was offset by carrying freight for other Cork firms. At the end of August an unusual cargo was forced upon it when the *Cheviot* was commandeered at Tralee by the National Army and made carry the bodies of two dead officers to Cork. (The company decided to charge the Provisional Government for the service rendered, and was duly sent £25 for its trouble.) In November a smaller and faster vessel, the *Clint*, was chartered to replace the *Cheviot* and its work was supplemented by a number of smaller vessels which were hired as the need arose to supply west Cork. The *Clint* was handed back in December 1922 owing to an offer from another company, Dowdall's, to take stout to Tralee at more economic rates.

Motor Fleet Expanded

The transport problem was further eased by the decision in August 1922 to purchase six new

Mallow Bridge, County Cork, following its destruction by Republican forces in 1922.

90

Prayers being said over the remains of General Michael Collins on board the steamer *Classic*, berthed at the quays in Cork before carrying his body to Dublin. Collins, Commander-in-Chief of the Irish National Army, was killed in a Republican ambush in West Cork in August 1922.

lorries. The company's engineer travelled to Liverpool late in the month and acquired four six ton and two four ton vehicles from Leyland, at a cost of £1,225 and £1,080 each respectively. This increased the brewery's fleet to ten and eased its problems significantly. The difficulties caused by railway disruption and high charges, and the non-return of empties, were overcome, and there was great satisfaction at being able to deliver supplies and collect empties 'at our own pleasure'. The new transport era had now begun in earnest, symbolised by the covering in and resurfacing of the old stable yard in preparation for its transformation into a garage for the new motor fleet. This work was completed in February 1923.

Interference with deliveries continued and in November 1922 three drivers and six lorry men were given conditional notice due to lorries being prevented from delivering in county areas by the IRA. Many of the brewery's lorries were commandeered by the National Army, and in January 1923 it was decided to charge them £10 per day for the six tonners, £7 for the four tonners and £5 for the three-and-a-half ton Fiat. Later in the month Murphy's was represented in a deputation from the Cork Motor Vehicle Owners which complained to the army about the manner in which vehicles were taken by them. In February the army returned the brewery's Ford car which had been taken by Republicans earlier in the month. It was in such a bad state that it was decided to scrap it and buy a closed-in Ford sedan to replace it. The Civil War ended in April-May 1923 (with victory for the pro-Treaty side) and Murphy's was subsequently compensated for damaged and lost vehicles and also for stout which had been taken while *en route* to Mallow and Kilmallock by thirsty Republicans.

In December 1922, several months before the ending of the Civil War, the Irish Free State had come into being. This marked the beginning of a new era in the history of Ireland, and in the history of James J. Murphy & Co. Ltd and Lady's Well Brewery.

J.J. MURPHY & CO's LTD

FAMOUS

STOUT

LADY'S WELL BREWERY, CORK

7

Between Wars

The Economy of the Irish Free State

We can only trust in better times to come.
Directors' Report, 1931

The fortunes of James J. Murphy & Co. Ltd in the decades between the end of the Civil War and the outbreak of the Second World War mirrored the vicissitudes of the Irish economy during that period. The creation of the Irish Free State and the partitioning of the six counties of Northern Ireland cut off the country's major industrial area in the northeast. The economy of the Free State was largely dependent on agriculture, and agricultural produce accounted for over 75 per cent of exports. Much of the rest was made up of products of agricultural origin such as whiskey and stout. The United Kingdom was virtually the only market for these exports and changes in market conditions there had a very immediate and significant impact on Irish producers.

In the new state almost two million of the country's three million population lived in rural areas and the majority of the workforce was engaged in agriculture. The First World War had been a great boon to agriculture in Ireland but by 1920 that success had begun to wane. Britain was in an economic depression and prices for agricultural produce were falling. This led to unemployment, poverty and emigration in Ireland which greatly affected rural areas, while not sparing urban centres.

The War of Independence and Civil War also left their legacy. Roads and railways in parts of the country were damaged and bridges destroyed. Many places of business were ruined when towns and cities had buildings destroyed. The centre of Cork city had been burned in December 1920. Payment of land annuities, rates and other taxes had been interrupted and there was pressure for the payment of those arrears with a consequent reduction in the amount of money in circulation, a situation not helped by the new Cumann na nGaedheal government's extremely conservative monetary policy.

These economic factors, both internal and external, impeded progress and combined with a carry-over of deep political division to make conditions in the new state very difficult. All businesses suffered and brewing was no exception.

Brewing in the Free State

The Irish Free State established its own independent customs and excise system but kept beer duty at 100s per barrel, a level it had reached in April 1920. Though duties had been reduced in Britain and in Northern Ireland in the 1920s, the Irish rate remained at 100s until the outbreak of the Second World War in 1939.

The brewers, distillers and vintners regarded this level of duty as too high. It was seen as overly punitive and 'nothing short of virtual prohibition'. They campaigned to have beer duty reduced to its pre-1914 level of 7s 9d per barrel 'to enable the working man to get his pint of beer

at the old price'. The fall in the number of operating breweries and distilleries was seen as the result of unjust taxation.

Vintners were also outraged at the restrictions on the opening hours of their premises. During the First World War restricted opening had been introduced to help the war effort by limiting the drinking opportunities of the workforce. These restrictions were inherited by the new state and were reinforced in 1924 with the passing of the Intoxicating Liquor Act. The conservative climate of the new Ireland rather than the pressures of a war effort was the motivation now.

A Liquor Commission was set up in 1925 to look into all aspects of the drinks trade. James J. Murphy & Co. Ltd was worried because, according to Albert St John Murphy, chairman, 'the tied house system was violently attacked by Cork traders, many of them our own tenants'. The Commission, however, was swayed by the brewers' lobby 'not seeing its way to interfere with the principle of legal contract and which verdict finished the resistance of the Cork [Vintners'] Society'.

The Commission's findings led to the passing of a new Act in 1927 which, amongst other things, reduced the number of public or licensed houses. Murphy's brewery lost thirteen city and ten country houses, some fully tied and others free but trading with the brewery. These losses did not unduly worry the firm as those of its houses closed were 'either the really redundant ones or the poor class and not over reputable houses and in many cases the value for letting would be greater without licence'.

Trade and Profits

The output of the brewery declined steadily through the 1920s and 1930s. By 1924 sales had fallen to under 60,000 barrels, less than half their First World War level. Seven years later, in 1931, the figures stood at 30,000 and reached a record low in 1935 of only 23,000 barrels. This pattern of declining sales was not peculiar to James J. Murphy & Co. Ltd. All Irish breweries suffered a fall in sales in this period also. Trade picked up a little again in the late 1930s but the upturn was not greatly significant. Sales in 1939 were only about 25,000 barrels.

In 1923 and 1924 the company made nett profits of over £67,000, the highest in the brewery's history. In those two years dividends of 11 per cent and 12 per cent were paid to shareholders and £50,000 was added to the company's reserves. Profits fell to £41,000 in 1925 and to £21,000 in 1926 and 1927. The company did not record a loss in any year in this period and annual dividends of between 5 per cent and 10 per cent were paid.

Though sales were falling at the time, these profits were being made due to the falling price of raw materials and cheaper wage and other costs. The annual wage bill of the brewery fell from an average of over £30,000 during the

1920s to an average of a little over £19,000 in the 1930s.

The profits of the good years had not been squandered. Though relatively good dividends were paid to shareholders, a significant reserve was also accumulated. In 1930 this stood at £230,000. Outstanding debentures were also redeemed with a consequent reduction in interest payments as well as a clearing of the original debt. The company thus managed to maintain itself in the harsh trading conditions of these two decades.

Changing Tastes

During the 1920s the change in consumer taste from porter to stout accelerated, especially in Cork city. The last year that the weaker, slightly cheaper porter was sold in the city was 1926. Porter continued to be sold in country districts, however, but in greatly decreasing quantities. Country sales of porter amounted to over £33,000 in 1927 but had fallen to under £10,000 by 1931. The fall continued in succeeding years and porter was last supplied to the country houses in 1943. Occasional brewings of porter were made in the years after 1943 for

consumption during the harvest months of August and September, but quantities were quite small.

City and Country

There was also a change in this period in the relative importance of the city and country trade. In the years of the First World War and its immediate aftermath, when agricultural prices were high, the country trade was far more significant than that of the city. Between 1914 and 1921 country sales were about double those of the city. As the 1920s advanced and the agricultural slump began to have a greater effect, this position changed. While total sales declined, those in the country districts fell more drastically, halving between 1923 and 1926. From 1929 city sales were greater than those of the country and this continued to be the position in later years. The company's directors were so worried by this decline that at the end of 1934 they reported to shareholders that 'the country trade to agencies and direct customers is rapidly tending to disappear altogether'.

REASONS FOR DECLINE

Economic Conditions

The overall decline in trade and the lessening in the importance of the country trade must be seen against the economic and social conditions of the time. James J Murphy & Co. Ltd had a limited export trade and almost all its Irish trade was relatively local in nature, done in the southern parts of the country, especially in Cork city and county and parts of counties Limerick and Kerry. These areas suffered more than most from the difficulties caused by the military activity and

the harvest months of August and September. Nature, in the form of bad weather and poor harvests, and economics, as manifested in more competitive markets and falling prices, combined to diminish sales. A brewery director noted in 1928: 'We have always found that bad weather has a detrimental effect on the consumption of stout and porter'. The scarcity of money due to low prices for cattle and crops, and poor harvests caused by bad weather are frequently mentioned in the directors' reviews of trading in the 1920s and 1930s.

Economic War

In 1932 there was a change of government and the new Fianna Fáil administration under Éamon de Valera entered into an 'economic war' with Britain. The new government refused to pay land annuities, due to Britain as a result of the division and purchase of large estates by former tenant farmers under the various Land Purchase Acts. Britain retaliated by placing protective tariffs on agricultural produce from Ireland. All areas of agriculture were hit and the already hard-pressed rural community faced even greater hardship. Though the tariff war eased somewhat in 1935, it lasted up to 1938 when it formally ended with the signing of the Anglo-Irish agreement on defence, finance and trade.

civil unrest of the 1919-23 period. The business of market towns had been badly affected. Cattle fairs were curtailed or cancelled. The movement of goods and people was restricted by damage to roads and railways. Curfews and fear led to a reduced social life and public houses were limited in their opening hours. Sales of the brewery's products suffered and distribution to agencies and direct customers was made difficult.

Agricultural Depression

Murphy's principal market area was largely rural and heavily dependant on agriculture. This agricultural dependence applied also in Cork city, where many were employed in the handling, processing or transport of agricultural produce. The slump in agricultural prices from 1920 reduced the amount of money circulating in rural areas and left farmers and farm labourers with less to spend. The brewery's income from its rural trade fell from over £400,000 in 1921, to £177,000 in 1926, and to £97,000 in 1932.

As noted earlier, city trade also fell during this period, but not so rapidly. Porter, and later stout, was the drink of the agricultural worker and brewery sales reached their annual peak in

An Taoiseach, Éamon de Valera visiting the Ford plant in Cork in 1936, during the economic war.

Ford workers at the Cork plant in 1930.

Emigration

Emigration during this period of almost two decades of economic difficulty was another factor in falling sales. It was mainly the young and potentially productive who left. Money was sent back to families in Ireland, but in their departure, the brewery directors saw the disappearance of future customers.

In their annual reviews of trade in this period the tone of the brewery directors is generally pessimistic: 'anxious for the future', 'no relief in sight', 'trade wretchedly slow', 'we are still awaiting the turn of the tide' and 'the whole situation is most unsatisfactory' typify the comments made in almost every one of those years.

HIGHS AND LOWS

Rebuilding

In the early years of the new state the rebuilding of the destroyed parts of Cork city led to increased employment in the building trade and was viewed by the brewery as beneficial to its trade. Increased house-building on the city's outskirts and the building of the new City Hall

and School of Comerce in the early 1930s were also regarded as important in that manual labourers engaged in such schemes were key consumers of Murphy's. A fall in the brewery's city trade in 1930 was partly attributed to a builders' strike which left about 1,000 out of work for three months.

Henry Ford & Son Ltd

In the late 1920s the Murphy directors saw the factory of Henry Ford & Son Ltd in Cork as another source of prosperity for the city and the brewery. The factory had begun production in 1919 and was one of the largest industrial concerns in the country. In its first years tractors, called Fordsons, were manufactured but in the mid-1920s production shifted to car assembly. In 1929 the factory changed again to tractor production and became the world's largest tractor factory, employing over 6,000 workers in the peak years of 1929 and 1930. A 7 per cent jump in the brewery's city trade in 1929 was noted by the directors as 'due entirely to Fordson's works - employing close on 7,000 men and which have been a tremendous asset to Cork, more especially since concentrating on the manufacture of tractors; at present their wages bill must run to over £30,000 per week'.

In the first half of 1930 over 15,000 tractors were manufactured at the Cork factory, but the market collapsed in the second part of the year. The Ford plant laid off most of its employees and this, coupled with a builders' strike in the city, caused stout sales to fall again. The hope that this industry had generated just a year before quickly dissipated. At the end of 1931 the Murphy's directors noted: 'The shortness of work in this big concern [Ford's] has had a great deal to do with the present depression in the city and surroundings and unfortunately there does not appear much prospect of their getting back to what they were a couple of years ago'.

In 1932 tractor production was transferred to Dagenham in England and many of the Cork employees emigrated to work at the new plant. The Cork factory returned again to car assembly but the earlier levels of employment were never again achieved.

The Shannon Scheme

The building of a hydroelectric dam on the river Shannon at Ardnacrusha between 1925 and 1929 was the biggest building and engineering project ever undertaken in Ireland and was referred to as the 'Eighth Wonder of the World' in newspapers of the time. The German company Siemens won the building contract and employed both German and Irish workers. The workers' canteens, serving over 1,000 men, were seen as lucrative outlets by the brewery, and the Murphy agent in the area, Mr Taylor, secured the contract to supply the Irish canteen. Fifty barrels of stout and 300 cases of bottled stout per week were supplied from the brewery's depot in Kilmallock.

Cork Industrial and Agricultural Fair

In 1931 the output of the brewery had dropped to 30,000 barrels and there was 'no apparent sign of any real improvement'. The directors' hopes that the Ford factory would give an economic boost to the city and to the brewery were not realised and they looked again for hopeful signs, sometimes grasping at straws. In 1932 the Industrial and Agricultural Fair was held in Cork and the directors hoped that this local event

would be of direct benefit to the brewery. James J. Murphy & Co. Ltd took a stand at the fair and invested in extra advertising. The fair ran from May to September but had a negative effect on trade, in the opinion of the chairman: 'Few strangers came and locals spent their spare cash on side shows and other entertainments.'

Sweeps, Pictures and Motor-cycles

In relaying the annual trade reviews to shareholders, the directors sometimes showed their displeasure at the changing tastes of the public, especially of the young. In 1930 the first Irish Hospitals' Sweepstake was held and they commented: 'These [Sweepstakes] have now taken their place along with the "Pictures" and similar amusements in attracting a larger share of the money which might otherwise have come

A 1930 newspaper advertisement for the Sweepstakes. 'Sweep fever', along with other 'amusements' like cinema, was seen as a threat to the brewery's trade.

98

in the direction of the trade.' The following year this 'sweep fever' was again decried.

Cinema was in its heyday in the 1930s and, along with dancing, was the subject of episcopal denunciation and state control because of the dangers posed to the moral fibre of Irish youth. The directors of James J. Murphy & Co. Ltd shared the displeasure of church and state at these modern pursuits, though they were motivated by more mundane concerns. The following comments were made by the company chairman in his annual reviews of trade:

A hectic and probably unsavoury talkie picture or a joy-ride on a motor-cycle being more to the taste of the younger generation than a pint of stout or porter. (1933)

A drowsy and uncomfortable bar room has but small attraction for many of them [younger people] compared to the delights of a joy-ride on a motor-cycle with an adequately filled side-car attachment or an erotic display of Hollywood charms at the local picture palace. (1934)

The tendency among the younger generation is now mainly towards softer and less exciting drinks and the doubtful pleasures of the local picture palace and dance hall. (1935)

Johnny Jump Up

I went into a bar and I called for a stout.
Says the barman, 'I'm sorry, all the beer is sold out.
Try whiskey or brandy, ten years in the wood'.
Says I, 'I'll try cider, I heard it was good'.

Oh never, oh never, oh never again,
If I live to be a hundred or a hundred and ten,
For I fell to the ground and I couldn't get up
After drinking a quart of that Johnny Jump Up.

(Lines from the Cork ballad, 'Johnny Jump Up')

In 1938 a cider, known colloquially as 'Johnny Jump Up', threatened Murphy's sales and the directors' irritation is apparent in this extract from their annual report of that year:

During the late Spring and Summer we were faced for the first time with what looked likely to develop into a serious menace. This took the form of a brand of Cyder from Clonmel, sponsored by the well known English firm of Bulmers . . . By what looked to be too opportune for a mere coincidence, it made its appearance in the city just as the Cork stout drinkers were feeling a bit peeved at the increase in price of the local article . . . The local topers took to it like ducks to water, none the less readily because it possessed a 'kick' that no mere stout could possibly hope to rival . . . The craze died down nearly altogether during the winter months and it remains to be seen whether the beverage will boom again during the coming summer.

This cider had many advantages. Its alcohol content was almost double that of stout but it was liable for mineral water duty of only 12s per barrel, compared to 100s for stout. It was thus sold at a much cheaper price than stout.

In 1939 anxiety eased as it was felt 'the public taste was being weaned from it or else that its attractions were being exploited in districts where it did not compete so directly with our product'.

Advertising

The question of advertising frequently vexed the directors of James J. Murphy & Co. Ltd. It was generally felt that their stout and porter advertised themselves. In 1892, as quoted earlier, a director said: 'We do not hope to thrive on pushing and puffing; our sole grounds for seeking popular favour is the excellence of our product.' Despite this, however, the firm did advertise in a limited way. During the late 1800s and early 1900s advertisements occasionally appeared in the Cork newspapers. These had little or no graphic content and advertised stout in the main. They were produced jointly with bottlers and wholesalers.

The brewery also advertised with show-cards or posters. These were displayed at railway stations, on street hoardings and in public houses. In the 1920s advertising 'show plates' were rented at the Cork Athletic Grounds and at Turner's Cross football ground. Advertising was also done in theatres and cinemas by way of curtain advertisements and slides. The company advertised by these means at the Palace Theatre and Imperial and Blackpool cinemas in Cork city, and in cinemas elsewhere in the Murphy's market area.

MURPHYS' STOUT "ON TOP"

QUALITY

Brewed solely from the choicest Hops and finest Irish Malt.

Bottled at the Brewery perfect in flavour and condition.

QUALITY TELLS

In 1927 the brewery paid £35 to advertise on the reverse of 700,000 tickets of the buses of the Cork Motorways Company. This firm ran services between the city and Bandon, Fermoy and Macroom. An opportunity to advertise on the tickets of the city's tramway company at the rate of 4d per thousand was refused in 1920, though this medium had previously been used. Advertisements were also taken in occasional publications. A full page in the 1919 directory of the Cork Chamber of Commerce cost £12. In 1928 £10 was paid for an advertisement in the *Excise Year Book*. A director noted: 'Price exorbitant but thought it prudent not to refuse.' Advertisements also appeared in the *Holly Bough*, the Christmas magazine of the *Cork Examiner* newspaper, theatre and sports programmes.

Many of the brewery's tied houses had the legend 'James J. Murphy & Co's Famous Stout and Porter' rendered in plaster on their gables or street frontages. These were permanent advertisements and a number of examples are still visible on public houses in Cork city and county.

Newspapers

Up to 1924 advertising had been carried out on a relatively ad hoc basis, but in that year it was decided to embark on a more organised and sustained campaign in an attempt to stem rapidly falling sales. The new advertisements appeared principally in the *Cork Examiner*, but also in the *Southern Star* and in sports and theatre programmes. Initial reaction was positive and the chairman noted at year's end: 'So far we are quite satisfied that we are being benefited by it and expect even more satisfactory results in the future.' In the five years prior to 1924 the total spending on all forms of advertising averaged under £300 per year. In 1924 this rose to £1,116 and stayed at those levels for the following three years, the duration of the campaign.

The new advertisements had a greater graphic content and used a variety of images. One, from 1925, featured a bottle of Murphy's Stout with the legends 'Support Local Manufacture, Quality Tells' or 'Nothing Succeeds like Success'. 'Bottled at the Brewery' featured prominently also. The brewery had installed a bottling plant in 1921 and was very proud of its bottled stout. This gained quite a good reputation as quality was maintained at a level not always achieved when bottling was done by publicans or wholesalers. Variations on the bottle theme appeared later.

Draught stout was promoted in advertisements with an image of a barrel of stout. One legend, 'Ask for it and see that you get it!' arose out of a practice in some public houses where the

MURPHYS' STOUT
STILL WINNING

On draught and in bottle
perfect in flavour and condition.

Made solely from the choicest Hops
and finest Irish Malt.

barman 'passed off' another stout to the customer in place of that requested. In an advertisement that ran in 1927 the bottle and barrel appear with a suggestion that barley growers protect their livelihoods by drinking Murphy's, which was brewed 'solely from Irish grown barley'. A general election was held in June of that year and the heading 'No 1 Preference' was added, giving the advertisement a current appeal.

The image of Eugen Sandow raising the horse (see pp. 104-105) appeared frequently and was sometimes combined with bottles of stout. A sporting theme figured in another advertisement that usually appeared in the sports pages of the *Cork Examiner*: 'ON AND OFF THE SPORTS FIELD. Half Time, Full Time, Every Time, Ask for Murphy's Stout'. This featured frequently in sports programmes of the period and a variant was used in theatre programmes.

In January 1927 the range of newspaper advertisements was enlarged with the addition of five new creations. The brewery directors felt that these would 'prove to be more up-to-date and effective', as the the advertising of the previous

two years did not produce the anticipated results. The new images were more imaginative. One showed a footballer scoring a goal with the words 'MURPHY'S STOUT Still Winning'. Another had a bottle of stout on a mountain top with a Quality flag and the legend 'MURPHY'S STOUT ON TOP'. A play on words also figured in another of the new advertisements: 'A Stout Supporter!' over the image of a man carrying a case of bottled stout. The fourth showed a crowd 'All Going for Quality', entering a public house, while the last had an image of a rather dandyish man, in a bow-tie, admiring a glass of stout.

The newspaper campaign ended quite suddenly in December 1927 when the directors noted: '*The Cork Examiner* advertising rates considered to be entirely too high. It was decided to withdraw all ours from that paper for the present.' They felt that the advertising had done little to improve sales and this is borne out by the

A 'stout' supporter!
of
MURPHY'S STOUT
Brewed solely from the choicest Hops
and finest Irish Malt.

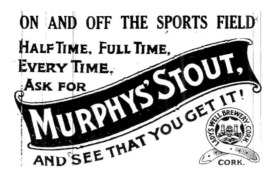

fact that sales fell by 35 per cent between 1924 and 1927, the period of the campaign.

In the 1925-7 period the local rival, Beamish & Crawford, advertised in the newspapers also and it was usual for the advertisements of the competing breweries to appear on facing pages.

While some of the Murphy's advertisements may seem somewhat innocent to the modern eye, in the context of their time they were quite innovative. The sustained campaign, with the added ingredient of competition from a rival concern, stimulated creativity and imagination. In the area of such advertising Murphy's was ahead of Guinness, in whose shadow it frequently struggled. The Guinness advertisements that coined the slogans 'Guinness is Good for You' and 'Guinness for Strength' and introduced the toucan, seal and other animal characters did not begin to appear until the end of the 1920s in Britain.

The Eve of War

In spite of almost twenty years of difficulty James J. Murphy & Co. Ltd had survived. Survival alone in the circumstances described was, in a way, an achievement and the cessation of the 'economic war' in 1938 gave cause for hope. The quality of Murphy's stout had been maintained and with the long-awaited economic upturn the brewery expected to benefit from the increased spending power of the consumer. In Europe, however, the storm clouds were gathering and world events were about to impinge on the Murphy's story once more.

EUGEN SANDOW (1867-1925)

Eugen (sometimes Eugene) Sandow was the stage name of Frederick Muller. He was born in Kaliningrad in the Russian Federation (formerly Konigsberg, eastern Prussia) on 2 April 1867. From an early age he devoted himself to exercise and body-building. He became an accomplished gymnast, wrestler and weightlifter and in 1891 became the world weight-lifting champion. He toured in Europe, America, Britain and Ireland as a 'strongman' and entertained audiences with feats of strength. His show involved bending iron bars, lifting pianos and horses.

He promoted the notion of health through exercise and physical fitness and wrote a very successful book, *Physical Strength and How to Obtain It* in 1897, to further his ideas. This was a bestseller in its time and even featured on the bookshelf of Leopold Bloom, hero of James Joyce's *Ulysses*. According to Joyce, in the Ithaca episode of that novel, Sandow's exercises were

designed particularly for commercial men engaged in sedentary occupations, were to be made with mental concentration in front of a mirror so as to bring into play the various families of muscles and produce successively a

he become that Sandow was known to many as the 'Murphy Man'. This visual association between strength and stout was being used by Murphy's almost forty years before Guinness first ran its 'Guinness for Strength' posters.

pleasant rigidity, a more pleasant relaxation and the most pleasant repristination of juvenile agility.

In 1898 Sandow founded the periodical *Physical Culture* and he also opened an academy or institute in London to teach others his methods.

Eugen Sandow performed in Ireland and was persuaded by the brewery to endorse Murphy's Stout. The famous image was then created: Eugen Sandow, the strongman, in weightlifter's garb, raising a horse above his head. The advertisements and bottle labels that carried this image also displayed his endorsement: 'From experience I can strongly recommend Messers J J Murphy's Stout. Dec 15th 1892.' This image was registered as a brewery trade mark and became synonymous with Murphy's in a short time. It has been used over the past century on a wide range of advertising and promotional material, sometimes in a quite stylised form. So familiar did

Eugen Sandow died on 14 October 1925 having injured himself lifting a motor car out of a ditch single-handedly.

In January 1926 another strong-man, Alex Kaas, who used the stage name Samson, visited Lady's Well Brewery. Charles Murphy, known as 'Young Mr Charlie' and a son of Charles Eustace Murphy, befriended him following a performance in Cork. Young Mr Charlie had successfully accepted Samson's challenge to the audience to bend an iron bar. After the show he invited Samson and his manager to visit the brewery. A directors' minute records that the guests proposed a 'photo opportunity'. Samson was to hang from a crane, holding a barrel of Murphy's Stout suspended from his teeth. The directors, however, 'found the matter not practicable and declined with thanks'. They presented Samson with a silver mounted blackthorn stick as a souvenir of his visit.

COOPERS AND COOPERING

The Lady's Well coopers in the mid-1920s.

The crest of the Cork Coopers' Society

The ancient craft of coopering was central to the development of brewing as an industry. Basically, coopering involves the making of casks or circular wooden containers of joined staves, bound together by hoops of wood or iron, and fitted with a head and bottom (or, strictly speaking, two heads).

The importance of coopering as a trade in Cork was established in the eighteenth century, when the city was enjoying its heyday as one of the main provisioning centres of the British empire. Wooden casks were used to pack many products, particularly meat and butter. The growth of brewing and distilling added to the demand for coopers, and they became numerically the second largest trade in the city after the shoemakers. The decline in the provisioning and butter trades during the nineteenth century, and the substitution of machine-made butter boxes for the traditional hand coopered firkin, had a serious impact on the trade. While in 1830 there had been 700 coopers in Cork, by 1900 their numbers had fallen to less than 300. They came to rely increasingly on breweries and distilleries, which did not provide enough work to employ even half of the city's coopers.

The coopers of the city were organised into the Cork Coopers' Society, which regulated the conditions of the trade and looked after the welfare of its members and their families. The society, like the other skilled trades societies, operated a 'closed-shop' policy which protected their employment and restricted it to their own members. Entry into a cooperage (as the workshop was known) for an apprentice was reserved for sons of coopers, while a non-member of the society or a cooper from outside Cork had to pay a joiner fee and could only apply for a position when all out-of-work members were employed.

The coopers' pay was set in 1872 at 36s for a six day week; their daily hours were from 6 a.m. to 6 p.m. in the summer months, and from 'light to dark' in the winter. Their pay was upped to 39s in April 1914, and this was followed by a succession of bonuses and wage increases which were demanded in order to meet the rising cost of living during the First World War. By 1920 the flat rate for coopers at Lady's Well Brewery was £4 17s for a five-and-a-half day week, while they now also enjoyed an annual paid holiday of one week.

The cooperage at Lady's Well was originally situated within the brewery proper, but was moved to the opposite side of Leitrim Street later in the nineteenth century. Frank Casey, who started in the brewery as an apprentice cooper in 1948, describes the cooperage as having been 'like a big stable or film set . . . Each cooper had his own block which was a piece of a tree trunk. That space was sacrosanct. There was an anvil between each two blocks . . . and various hoops and tools hung on the walls.' The great majority of the casks used by the brewery were manufactured by its own coopers, who also repaired damaged casks. They formed the biggest single group of workers in the brewery, with up to three dozen coopers being employed in the days before the First World War. Wartime restrictions saw the numbers drop to a low of twenty in 1918. It rose again to twenty-nine in 1924, but six were discharged in 1925, and the numbers remained at around this level (mid-twenties) over the following decades until the early 1960s.

The coopers were highly skilled and highly paid and enjoyed their status as the 'aristocrats of labour'. Their dress and demeanour always set them apart from other workers. Frank Casey remembers the coopers' 'uniform' of 'a bowler hat, a white shirt and tie, a dark navy suit and a pair of highly polished boots. When they got to work they took off the jacket an put on a white apron . . . and over the apron a shorter apron made from a hop pocket' (the bags in which the hops were delivered to the brewery). He recalls the disapproval of the older coopers at the wearing of overalls in later years, and at the refusal of the younger coopers to wear the traditional bowler hats.

The introduction of metal casks in the early 1960s marked the beginning of the end of the brewery's association with coopering. The metal casks, and subsequently the now familiar cylindrical kegs, gradually supplanted the old wooden casks in the mid-1960s. Ornamental wooden barrel shaped covers for the brewery's first dispensers were made by the soon-to-be displaced coopers, who also did some repair work and manufactured items such as cocktail cabinets. When metal completely replaced wood in 1967, the Lady's Well coopers either retired or were given jobs in other areas of the brewery such as the dispatch office and the bottling store. The cooperage was closed down, and the long association of this traditional craft with the brewery came to an end.

Lady's Well coopers at work.

8

The Emergency and Post-War Years

The Emergency

The Second World War (or 'the Emergency', as it was known in Ireland) began in September 1939 and, although Ireland was neutral, the war impacted heavily on economic and social life in the state. This was particularly so from 1941 as shortages of fuel, raw materials and other items resulted in the closure of many factories. Brewing was one of those industries which was able to maintain production, but not without difficulty. While trade was not hurt, costs of all materials rose, many were unobtainable, taxes were increased, and plant renewal and extension was impossible.

Taxes and Supplies

Duty increases were the first enemy with which James J. Murphy & Co. Ltd had to contend after the outbreak of war, as the government sought to strengthen its reserves for the uncertain times ahead. An additional 12s per barrel of beer, or a halfpenny per pint, was imposed. Following lengthy discussions between Murphy's and their fellow Cork brewers of Beamish & Crawford, it was decided not to pass the extra charge on to the consumer but to divide it between the brewer and the publican. Increases in income tax and corporation tax added to the company's burden.

For the first year of the war, the three essential materials of barley, hops and coal were still readily available, though their cost had inevitably begun to rise. Wages were increased under an agreement with the trade unions at the

brewery, but these costs were counterbalanced by savings in the areas of house repairs and 'carriage and commission'. As well as this, the company was surprised by a sudden upsurge in trade in the first six months after the outbreak of war. All in all, nett profits (a large portion of which were kept in reserve), were up by £3,450.

The following year saw the exigencies of wartime begin to bite a little harder. Barley prices were more than double what they had been five years earlier, while the threat of German U-boats in the Atlantic pushed the cost of freight and insurance on American hops (which were favoured over the English variety) to 'alarming heights'. The price of coal, imported from Britain, also rose. While petrol became scarcer, the shortage did not yet interfere with business. Income tax rose again, while a further half–penny per pint increase in beer duty was absorbed, as in 1939, by the brewers and publicans. All of these factors led to a drop in profits of £5,000 and a reduction in the quarterly dividend from 5 to 4 per cent in 1940.

Decline in City Trade

The company's subsidiaries in Bandon and Kilmallock continued to return satisfactory figures, which reflected the general situation whereby trade in rural areas remained strong, while that in the city of Cork had, in the words of the chairman, 'deteriorated to an alarming extent. One only has to walk down any of the principal quays of the city to realise this and it

109

can be no surprise to anyone when we remember that the normal trade of the city has been virtually closed down and what an increase of unemployment and poverty must result.' Meanwhile, the war impacted in a direct way on the company when the offices of its auditors, Wheeler & Co., were completely destroyed during one of the Luftwaffe's bombing raids on London. (James J. Murphy & Co. Ltd, in common with other Irish firms, retained the services of London auditors because, apparently, the discretion of Irish auditors was questioned by the board. A firm of Irish auditors was finally appointed in 1967.)

Shortages Worsen

The year of 1941 saw shortages begin in earnest as the British government initiated a policy of 'silent' economic sanctions against Ireland, because of its continuing refusal to abandon its neutrality. Imported goods such as petrol, coal and hops became scarce, while the government tightened controls over Irish produced materials such as barley as the maintenance of essential supplies became a priority.

As happened during the First World War, beer gravities were reduced and a limit was put on the amount of malt which breweries were permitted to use. Malting was actually temporarily halted by order of the government at the beginning of the 1941 season, but a crisis in the industry was averted when the decision was reversed later in the year. The malt restrictions were lifted in 1942-3. American hops arrived for the last time during the war in 1941. The story of the last consignment's journey, according to the chairman, 'would require an epic poet to describe'; it all arrived safely, however, 'by

devious routes, whether round the North or South pole will never be known'. English hops were bought for the first time in many years as an insurance against not getting any more from the US and in order to get the company's name on the books of the British Board of Hop Control. In the following years hops were obtained, albeit at a high price, from Britain and were blended with the favoured American supplies until the latter ran out towards the end of the war.

Fuel

Both the quantity and quality of British coal dwindled dramatically. Irish turf replaced it for domestic use, but the use of turf for commercial purposes was forbidden and the brewery had to make do with the coal it had in reserve, what 'dribs and drabs' it could obtain from merchants,

and the primary native coal substitute which industry was permitted to use: timber. 'Huge quantities' of the latter were burnt 'at a frightful cost'. The fuel shortages had a wide-ranging impact as they began to hit the railways and electricity production. By 1943 the country had only 20 per cent of its petrol requirements, but, while its use for private transport was banned, sufficient quantities were made available, though never guaranteed, to the brewery to allow

Murphy's draymen
'Tucker' Lyons (left)
and Denis Lenihan
crossing St Patrick's
Bridge, Cork in 1943.

it to maintain its deliveries, in conjunction with horse and sea transport and a rather bizarre-looking gas fuelled lorry which had a huge baloon attached to it. The drinks trade was a fruitful source of revenue for the government, while the importance placed on the maintenance of beer supplies for morale purposes by governments was shown by an episode in 1942 which illustrated how official thinking had changed since the days of Lloyd George during the First World War.

'. . . at best a luxury and at worst a poison'

In the early part of that year the Irish government proposed to the British authorities an exchange of beer for wheat. The British refused and the Irish temporarily suspended the export of stout. An alarmed British Minister for Food minuted that 'The effect of this on the output of essential works in Belfast and other places will I fear be serious'. A deal was struck whereby beer exports were resumed in return for 20,000 tons of wheat. The American envoy in Dublin kept alive the spirit of Lloyd George, complaining to his British counterpart about this exchange of 'a vital necessity [wheat] for what Americans regard at best as a luxury and at worst a poison'!

Other Shortages

There was difficulty in securing a wide range of other materials which, although less essential than barley, hops and coal, were nevertheless basic requirements in the running of a brewery. The supply of oak staves for the manufacture and repair of casks gradually dwindled until, by 1944, the brewery's coopers were using timbers

for repairs which would normally have been burnt; iron hoops also became scarce. Sufficient quantities of bottles and crates were maintained, by continuing to use those which under normal circumstances would have been replaced. Alternative sources for some items were found, but at a cost; for example, by 1943 most of the brewery's crown corks for its bottles were coming from neutral Portugal (with which Ireland had a direct trading link) 'at an out-rageous price'. The overall priority was to secure all necessary supplies, regardless of the cost.

Trade and profits

Despite all the difficulties with production during the war years, sales and profits did not suffer. The directors' report for 1941 noted that there had been a good deal of spare money in circulation, partly as a result of increased employment due to the timber and turf drive, and partly from the thousands of emigrants who, since the beginning of the war, had flocked across the channel to work in Britain's war industries and fight in its armed forces. In the words of the chairman, 'some of the surplus of our temporary émigrés is finding its way back to the south of Ireland'. This remained the case for the rest of the Emergency. Trade was also increased during the war years

The staff and directors of the brewery at a dinner hosted by the former to celebrate the centenary of the firm in 1956. A presentation of Waterford glass was made to the directors, together with mahogany cases made by brewery workers. The last two surviving Murphys on the board are seated in the front row: chairman, Arthur William Murphy is fifth from the left and John Fitzjames (The Colonel) is fourth from the left.

by the large scale mobilisation of thousands of men into the auxiliary defence and security forces (the LDF and LSF), as well as by the limitations on Guinness supplies caused by the increasing restrictions on rail transport.

Profits for the year 1941 were further enhanced by the substantial drop in duty paid owing to the considerable reduction in gravity imposed by government order. Due to the restrictions, Murphy's, along with all the other brewers, could not produce enough beer to meet the demand in certain areas and for certain periods during 1942. The restrictions had ended by 1943 and trading results and profits were good. The quarterly dividend paid to share-holders, which had been reduced from 5 to 4 per cent in 1940 was restored to 5 per cent again by the payment of a 1 per cent bonus.

The upturn continued in 1944, and the results of that year's trading were, the share-holders were told, 'highly satisfactory'. Output

was up 4,155 (32 gallon) barrels on 1943 and profits rose by £4,030 giving a healthy total of £53,010. A bonus dividend of 2 per cent was paid, or a total of 6 per cent.

POST-WAR YEARS

Peace and (temporary) Prosperity

The ending of the war in Europe in May 1945 brought 'great relief and pleasure', and also a brief economic boom arising, just as after the First World War, from the release of pent-up consumer demand. James J. Murphy & Co. Ltd's output for the year 1945 was up 7,244 barrels on 1944; profits available for allocation showed an increase of £13,000 and a dividend of 7 per cent was paid. The increased trade continued into early 1946, but that year's overall figures showed a slight drop in sales from 1945. The drop was not sufficient to affect profits, however, and was more than balanced by a reduction in the standard rate of income tax from 7s 7d to 6s 6d in the pound.

The appalling weather of 1947 resulted in one of the worst harvests in living memory. The brewery was forced to buy foreign barley, and the import of Chilean and Australian barley saved the Irish brewing industry from disaster. The clouds did have a silver lining for the company, however, as sales of Murphy's stout received a major boost because of the weather-enforced curtailment of supplies of Guinness from Dublin. The rise in output of over 5,000 barrels was actually less than expected as the huge increase in duty of 3d per pint in October upset calculations and considerably curtailed trade for the last three months of the year. This price rise was among the factors which contributed to the defeat of Fianna Fáil, which had been in power for sixteen years, in the general election of February 1948. The new inter-party government, to the great relief of the brewing industry and drinking public, reversed the increase and this, together with the resumption of normal supplies from Dublin, saw Murphy's output return to its 1946 level.

Plant Renewal Resumed

The shortages did not end with the war; indeed, the scarcity of many goods in 1946 was, according to the chairman, 'even more noticeable than in the war years'. By 1947-8, however, most materials were readily available, though at a high cost. Plant and machinery renewal again became possible and by the end of 1949 the necessary replacements of old vessels, coolers, etc. was almost completed, the high cost being met by allocations made for the purpose during the Emergency years. The complete replacement of old wooden plant with aluminium or aluminium-lined vessels (a process which began before the First World War!) was finally completed by 1951. Other essential improvements at Lady's Well included the re-roofing and re-modelling of the bottling plant, while new bottling machinery was installed at the company's subsidiaries in Bandon and Kilmallock.

Declining Trade

Following the 'boom' in the late war and early post-war period, trade went into steady decline, a trend replicated in the brewing industry in the rest of Ireland and in Britain. Falling sales were allied to rising production costs, with everything from coal and petrol to wages and duties costing more, while the selling price of beer was kept down. In 1952 a 1d per pint increase was granted by the government, and this helped to offset the dramatic drop in sales in the region of 11 per cent occasioned by the 3d per pint duty increase imposed in that year's budget.

The 1950s in Ireland were years of economic stagnation, with steadily rising emigration and unemployment. Companies like James J. Murphy & Co. Ltd (small, family controlled firms producing small quantities for a protected home market), typical of the Irish industrial scene, were unable to respond. Technology and management practices had changed little by the time the company celebrated its centenary in

Dray leaving Lady's Well Brewery, 1953.

1956, and despite occasional good years like 1954, the overall picture was one of decline.

Boardroom Changes

The period from 1946 to 1958 saw major changes in the make-up of the board of directors of James J. Murphy & Co. Ltd, as the second generation of Murphys passed away. Fitzjames died in 1946, his place on the board taken the following year by his son, Lt. Col. John Fitzjames, better known as 'The Colonel'. Another son of James J., Charles Eustace, died in 1951. This was a significant event, as he had been the dominant figure in the firm for many years. On the death of his father in 1897 he became, according to the directors' reports, 'in fact, if not in name, the virtual Managing Director of the firm, and for well over fifty years exercised what I may call a "benevolent dictatorship" over the affairs of Lady's Well Brewery'. While his 'benevolent dictatorship' had carried the company through the first half of the twentieth century, his domination of the firm and failure to delegate decision-making impeded its continued development in wake of his death. Charles's brother, Albert St John, who had been company chairman since 1919, died the following year (ill health had limited his active involvement for some years previously) and was replaced as chairman by his nephew Arthur William Murphy, who was over eighty years of age and unlikely to be a symbol of rejuvenation for the company. On his death in 1958, the chairmanship passed to his cousin John Fitzjames Murphy, the Colonel, the only remaining Murphy on the board.

In 1951 Frank Horgan, the company secretary, had become the first non-family member to be given a seat on the board. The secretary, along with the head brewer, effectively ran the brewery on a day-to-day basis. The former was responsible for the administrative aspects of the business (tied houses, sales and marketing, trade union negotiations and so on) while the latter oversaw everything connected with the actual business of brewing (purchase of materials, malting, maintenance, quality control, etc.). Following the deaths of Albert St John and Major James E. Murphy (son of Charles Eustace) in 1952, John Quinlan, manager of the company's Kilmallock subsidiary was co-opted on to the board, followed by Joseph Brennan, the West Cork Bottling Co. manager, in 1953. When the latter resigned in 1957, his place as manager of the Bandon subsidiary was taken by Arthur Masson, the accountant at Lady's Well. Edward Cruise, the head brewer since 1948, was co-opted on to the board in the same year. Masson's successor as accountant and the assistant secretary, Michael Warner, took Arthur William Murphy's seat following his death in 1958, and John Riordan, the second brewer, was co-opted as an extra director in the same year. (John Riordan became head brewer in 1962.) Frank Horgan died in 1960 and his place on the board went to Arthur Masson, while Michael Warner became company secretary. In the same year Frank McCarthy-Murrogh, a nephew of Arthur Murphy's, also took a seat on the board.

While the commitment and dedication to duty of none of these men can be questioned, it could be argued that an opportunity was lost to appoint (as other firms had done) managerial expertise from outside the ranks of the family and company, individuals who might have brought new perspectives and badly needed creativity and dynamism at a crucial juncture in

Albert St. John Murphy (1859-1952), son of James J. Murphy and company chairman, 1919-1952.

Charles Eustace Murphy (1863-1951), son of James J. Murphy. From the time of his father's death in 1897, he was 'in fact, if not in name, the virtual Managing Director of the firm'.

the history of the brewing industry, and in the history of Irish economic and social life.

Tied Houses

The slackness of trade in the late 1950s saw a large number of the brewery's older tenants give up. Many of these were in the inner city area which in this period was undergoing depopulation due to the growth of new suburban housing developments. Murphy's adopted a policy of 'following the population out into the suburbs'. Old houses in the city centre were closed and the licences transferred to new pubs which were built in the suburbs. As well as capturing trade in these areas, the newly built premises were regarded as 'first-class advertisements' for the firm and its products. (See highlight, pp. 118-121).

Attempts to Extend Trade

Despite the company's building of new tied houses, and its upgrading of existing premises and the installation of new tenants, trade continued to decline. A decision was taken in 1963 to seek new trade in other parts of the country. Dublin, by far the largest market, had always been solid Guinness territory and James J. Murphy & Co. Ltd had never traded there. In the summer of 1963, however, Guinness, which had never had a tied house estate, adopted a new

policy of buying pubs with the object of gaining experience of the retail trade. Publicans in the capital reacted negatively to this new development, regarding it as a threat to their livelihoods. Murphy's were made aware that if its stout was made available in Dublin, many vintners would be glad to sell it. An agency was established there and on 1 October 1963 the first lorry load of bottled Murphy's stout left Lady's Well bound for the capital. Trade grew rapidly throughout the month, but the extent of Murphy's success led publicans to fear that it could prejudice the traditional and more lucrative Guinness draught trade. Consequently, they raised the price of Murphy's by 2d per pint, which resulted in the failure of the Dublin experiment almost as soon as it had begun. Compensation for this setback came with the sudden expansion of trade in Waterford in the same year. The bottled Murphy's was cheaper than its competitors in the area because of the fact that it was bottled at the brewery, thus eliminating the 'cut' taken by local bottlers.

Pint Bottles

The brewery had begun to bottle stout in pint bottles for the first time in 1959. This development had been resisted in the past for fear of harming the more profitable draught trade, but the continuing decline in the latter, allied to increasing requests from customers for pint bottles, left the board with little choice. It was felt that if the demand for stout in pint bottles was not met by Murphy's, its competitors would be only too pleased to step into the breach. The move proved successful as new business was won without causing any serious drop in the existing trade in draught and half-pint bottles.

The 'Iron Lung'

In 1961 another new development saw the introduction by the company of a number of metal casks. Since the foundation of the brewery

draught stout had been put into coopered wooden casks, in which it would mature or condition for up to two weeks. When the stout was ready, the casks were mounted on their sides on stands called stillions, about one-and-a-half feet off the ground, behind the pub counter. Glasses were filled by the publican through a tap which was inserted into the head of the cask. In larger premises, usually in the city, at least two casks were used simultaneously, one with highly conditioned stout and another with a lower, or flatter, brew. The publican would fill the glass about three quarters up from the high cask and top it up with flat beer from the lower cask. Smaller pubs, usually in rural areas, would use one barrel and fill jugs from it, while larger city pubs would have several casks tapped simultaneously, with skilled bar people achieving the perfect combination.

Throughout the 1950s Guinness had been gradually replacing wooden casks with new metal containers, which were kept horizontally

and pressurised by nitrogen and carbon dioxide. The metal casks were more economical because there was no need for the constant repairs and maintenance demanded by the old vessels. These new containers were more durable, sanitary and easily cleaned; they were also more easily handled and better consistency could be achieved. Guinness completed the changeover from wood to metal in 1961, and in that year Murphy's bowed to the inevitable and bought in a number of the 'iron lungs'. These were used for high stout, which was combined with low stout from wooden casks. For a period prior to this the company attempted to capitalise on public doubts about the virtue of stout from metal with advertisements bearing the slogan 'Murphy's From the Wood - That's Good!' It was quickly realised, however, that metal was even better and over the following four or five years the new barrel-shaped metal casks were introduced to all the brewery's houses, first in the city and later in the rural areas.

Much work was done by the brewing department, principally by chief chemist Pat Early, in developing and perfecting dispensing technology to ensure the best possible product from the metal casks. By 1962 a dispenser which compared very favourably with that developed by Guinness had been produced, and at about a third of the cost. A symbol of the transition to a new era was provided when the brewery's coopers, whose obsolescence was heralded by the metal cask, were commissioned to make small barrel-type covers or 'cowls' for the first dispensers. These ornamental fittings at counter height were a new development which had the added advantage of being an advertisement for the product.

1961. The brewery's city delivery store as the first consignment of metal casks are loaded for delivery.

A Cork family watches Éamon de Valera open the Irish television service, RTÉ, on New Year's Eve 1961. The Murphy's chairman, Colonel Murphy, saw the arrival of television as an unwelcome development because it would keep people out of the pubs.

Developments in the Brewing Industry

In the late 1950s and early 1960s Guinness underwent a rapid phase of expansion, and by 1964 all of the country's remaining breweries (outside of Cork) had either closed down or were taken over by that brewing giant. It had also attempted to buy Beamish & Crawford, but was beaten in a take-over battle by Canadian Breweries, which acquired the Cork brewery in 1962. An approach by Guinness to James J. Murphy & Co. Ltd was rebuffed and the company remained independent. The changes which the brewing industry was undergoing, however, posed new challenges to the old firm.

While stout was still by far the most popular beer in Ireland, the late 1950s and early 1960s saw the beginnings of changing tastes with the growing popularity of ale and lager, especially among the increasingly affluent younger generation. This affluence, and more cosmopolitan tastes, accompanied the programme of economic modernisation initiated under Seán Lemass, which saw the ending of protectionism and the opening up of the Irish economy. The social changes which accompanied this new economic era were accelerated by the advent of television. Irish television was launched on New Year's Eve

1961, and the arrival of televisions into the homes of Cork in 1962 was an unwelcome development in the eyes of the chairman, Lt. Col. John Fitzjames Murphy, just as cinema had been to his predecessors. The novelty of this new diversion kept people out of the pubs in the early months of 1962, while, more seriously, according to the chairman, 'the weekly payments of 10s or more, for renting or hiring television sets, represent in many cases the amounts which had previously been spent in licensed premises. It is too early yet', concluded the Colonel, 'to say how soon this phase will pass . . . '.

Guinness, with its newly acquired Irish breweries, trading agreements with British breweries, and expensive and innovative advertising, led the field in response to the changing tastes, offering young consumers ales such as Smithwicks and Phoenix, and Harp lager. Canadian Breweries, meanwhile, invested heavily in the Beamish & Crawford plant, extensively modernising it and converting it for the production of keg ale (Celebration) and lager (Carling Black Label).

James J. Murphy & Co. Ltd was forced to respond if it was to have a future, and the visit of a representative from British brewers Watney Mann in 1964 heralded the beginning of a new phase in the history of Lady's Well Brewery.

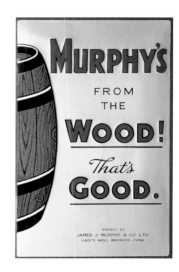

Legend on a former
Murphy's tied house on
Barrack Street, Cork.

TIED HOUSES

A tied house is a public house (pub) or licensed premises which, for one reason or another, is obliged to trade in the products of one brewery. Houses, as pubs were called by the breweries, became 'tied' in a variety of ways. In many cases the house was owned or held on a very long lease by the brewery, and let to a tenant at a monthly rent. In other cases the brewery owned the licence of the house, but not the property itself. On occasion a house became tied when the brewery bought a debt owed by the house owner to a rival brewery. In return for the favour, as it were, the publican agreed to deal exclusively with the new supplier. Publicans, trading in free or independent houses, sometimes established a tie in return

for financial help towards funding a redecoration or refurbishment, for example.

The nature of the tie varied. Most ties were complete, and the house could only sell products produced or supplied by its brewery. Other ties were for stout only, or perhaps for stout and ale. As part of the tie, the brewery was responsible for all repairs to and decoration of its tied houses.

The acquisition of estates of tied houses was a feature of the brewing industry in Britain, especially in the second half of the nineteenth century. In many cases these holdings numbered hundreds of houses. In Ireland, the tied house system was a feature of the trade only in the south of the country. After 1901, Murphy's and

Beamish & Crawford were the only breweries to operate the system. The two Cork breweries, the only remaining ones in the city, had about 200 tied houses each.

From 1856, when it first began brewing, James J. Murphy & Co. began to acquire tied houses. By 1860 the brewery owned sixteen houses and in the succeeding decades of growth this pace of acquisition was maintained. The brewery had a tie with 104 houses when it became a limited company at the end of 1883 and in 1901, following the acquisition of Sir John Arnott & Co.'s St Fin Barre's Brewery, its tied estate numbered in the region of 200. The majority of houses were in the city. In 1935, for example, Murphy's had 137 city and 40 country houses. In

Cork city the brewery had ten houses in North Main Street and eight in Parnell Place and in Shandon Street. Many other city streets had more than one Murphy's house also.

The purchase price of a house and its licence varied. In 1858 £600 was paid to a Mr John Baggott for No. 1 Union Quay and it was re-let to him at an annual rent of £50. This was one of the highest prices paid by Murphy's for a house in the nineteenth century. Usually a house and its licence cost less than £200. Significant amounts were invested in the acquisition of houses and a not insignificant expense was incurred in their maintenance. At the end of 1883 Murphy's tied houses and their trade were valued at £116,500. In the mid-1970s the tied house property (almost 150 houses) was valued at £750,000. The expenditure involved was

justified by a director of the company as follows: 'The sales in our Tied Houses constitute the absolutely essential foundation of our trade.'

A tied house estate guaranteed a brewery a market for its products and to a large extent protected it from competition. Murphy's and Beamish & Crawford in Cork preserved their trade through their ownership of tied houses while all other breweries in Ireland eventually closed down or were taken over by Guinness. Murphy's also regarded its tied houses as 'a standing advertisement'. In the later nineteenth and early twentieth centuries the legend 'James J. Murphy & Co.'s Famous Stout and Porter' appeared in large letters on the walls and gables of many of its houses. In 1967, when Murphy's was in partnership with Watney Mann, an effort was made to give the tied houses

Deanrock House in Togher, Cork, the last tied house opened by the brewery.

an up-to-date and uniform look. Rex Archer, then manager of the tied estate, travelled to Manchester in the company of William Harrington, a young Cork artist and designer. They were shown how the Wilson's Brewery (a subsidiary of Watney Mann) had achieved a 'look' for its tied houses and applied the same principles in Cork. A complete colour scheme was designed for each house and also a uniform lettering for the facia name plates. This lettering is still visible on many former Murphy's tied houses in the Cork area.

The tied house system also had disadvantages. While a level of protection from competition was afforded, there was a tendency towards complacency; a captive market did not encourage the development of aggressive marketing skills. In addition,

The Ovens Tavern,
Oliver Plunkett
Street, Cork.

large amounts of capital were tied up in the estates, capital which might otherwise have been used for investment in new markets and wider distribution, as well as in the development of new products. Without a tied estate, a brewery could have both the motivation and the capital to explore such possibilities.

The maintenance and decoration of premises, in addition to liability for rates, was always expensive and in the later 1950s and early 1960s customers began to demand more of their pub. Comfortable seating, lounges and more modern facilities were needed to satisfy the customer of these new, more affluent times. In 1966 a director noted that 'The public tend to patronize more and more the better houses and tend to bypass the many older ones with less comfortable amenities'. By the early 1970s the cost of maintenance and renovation of the tied estate was becoming greater than the return on their trade.

The monthly rents paid by the majority of tenants were subject to statutory control and in the later

1960s were at unrealistically low and unviable levels from the brewery's point of view. Attempts were made to re-negotiate leases with a view to increasing brewery revenue and funding necessary expenditure on the houses.

Tied house tenants made occasional attempts to free themselves of their tie. They made a submission to the Liquor Commission in 1925 to be allowed to trade freely, but were unsuccessful. In 1953 a commission was set up by the government to look into restrictive trade practices. The

tied house system, as operated by the Cork breweries, was examined but no changes were deemed to be necessary. Unhappy tenants were not averse to dealing quietly with a rival brewery and 'passing off' their products as those of their own brewer. Arising from such practices, early stout advertisements, in exhorting the public to drink a particular brand, frequently finished with the warning '. . . and see that you get it!'

The development of new suburbs on the outskirts of Cork city encouraged the brewery to build new tied houses in these areas in the late 1950s and over the following decade. In 1959 'The Tory Top' was built in the large new suburb of Ballyphehane. In 1961 'The Orchard' in Ballinlough was opened and in the following year the brewery built 'The Outpost' in Bishopstown. Others followed in the expanding northside suburbs of Gurranebraher and Farranree. In 1968 'Deanrock House' was opened in Togher; it was to be the last tied house built or acquired by Murphy's. These houses traded very profitably and well justified the large investment involved. At that time, with the decline of city centre living and the changes in the nature of employment, many city centre houses lost business and ceased trading. The redundant licences from a number of these houses were transferred to enable the opening of the new suburban pubs.

The brewery lost tied houses in a number of ways through the years. Four Murphy's houses were destroyed in the burning of Cork by British forces in 1920 (compensation was later paid for the losses incurred), while the number of brewery licences was reduced in 1927 with the passing of the Intoxicating Liquor Act. In 1964 the Catholic bishop of Cork, Cornelius Lucy, requested the permission of the brewery to demolish one of its tied houses to facilitate an extension to the city's Cathedral. The chairman of the company, Lt. Col. J. F. Murphy acceded to the request and informed share-holders that 'The compensation in this case, we are told, will not be paid until we reach the next world!'.

Other difficulties were also en-countered. Most tenants were proud of their premises and of their clientele. A valued Murphy's tenant in Cork complained frequently to the brewery about the adjoining premises, also a Murphy's house. The brewery records note the following regarding the house: *Small old-fashioned public bar, snug and tap-room in poor condition. It is a continual embarrassment to X, next door, because it has the reputation of being the haunt of prostitutes and tinkers. The Company tried to eject the tenant on the grounds that she ran an undesirable premises, but failed. Y lives there with her husband and assorted dogs and cats. She is dirty and completely unsuitable.*

Interestingly, given that the brewery itself was such a predomi-nantly male environment for most of its history and that women until recently were largely excluded from public life, a survey of tied house records across the years shows that a majority of tenants were women.

In the late 1960s Beamish & Crawford allowed Guinness to be sold in its tied houses. Many Murphy's tenants requested permission to do likewise but were refused. In June 1969 a reciprocal trading agreement was reached between the two Cork breweries. Beamish & Crawford allowed Murphy's Stout and Watney's Red Barrel into their 150 or so tied houses and in return Murphy's allowed Bass ale and Carling lager into theirs.

By 1973 the maintenance of the tied estate had become so expensive and the pressures from publicans to break the tie so strong that the brewery board decided to initiate the sale of some of its tied houses. Within a year a vintners' co-operative was running the brewery and the sale of tied houses became a matter of policy. By 1982, when the brewery went into receivership, most houses had been disposed of and in the following years the remaining sales were completed.

Cork artist William Harrington's original drawings from 1967 for the redesign of one of Murphy's tied houses, The High House on Blarney Street, Cork.

9

From Watney Mann to Receivership

Watney Mann

Watney Mann Ltd was one of the 'Big Six' British brewing conglomerates that emerged in the late 1950s and early 1960s. Its Red Barrel keg ale was being vigorously promoted in Britain and sold well in Dublin. A move to Ireland was considered, and as Beamish & Crawford had been acquired by Canadian Breweries and Guinness controlled all the other breweries, James J. Murphy & Co. Ltd was their only option if they were to acquire an Irish base.

Louis King, a director of Watney Mann and chairman of Wilson's Brewery, Manchester, one of the Watney Mann group of breweries, paid a visit to Lady's Well in the autumn of 1964 and made a timely offer to the Murphy's board. Watney's wanted an Irish brewery to produce its ale for the Irish market, North and South; in return Murphy's would have its old and outdated brewery modernised and improved, and would be in a position to compete in the diversifying and changing beer market with Beamish & Crawford and Guinness. An agreement was signed and approved by the shareholders in November and on 1 December 1964 King was appointed a director of James J. Murphy & Co. Ltd as a nominee of Watney Mann Ltd. The latter acquired a 30 per cent holding in Murphy's and invested an initial sum of £350,000 in Lady's Well Brewery.

Work began immediately on the construction of a new brewery for the production of Red Barrel ale, as well as for the improved production of Murphy's stout. A third company, Watney Mann (Ireland) Ltd was formed in June 1965, with directors from both Murphy's and Watney Mann, to control the marketing and sales of the new product on a national basis. While the reconstruction of Lady's Well was under way, Red Barrel was imported from London. As well as changes in the production side of the brewery, there was also a complete overhaul in the administrative side of the company, as office and accounting technology and procedures were modernised.

The partnership with Watney Mann heralded a new phase in the brewery's history, and hopes were high that a new era of prosperity had begun. By the end of the decade, however, these hopes had been dashed.

Red Barrel

Work on the new brewery began immediately, but problems were encountered from the beginning and delays slowed down the remodelling. Bad weather, foundation and drainage problems, and the shortage of skilled technicians and draughtsmen among the sub-contractors, all caused delays throughout 1965 and into 1966. Red Barrel was imported from England and was sold initially in Murphy's tied houses and subsequently more generally. Backed up by an advertising campaign aimed at white collar workers and 'rugby types', it quickly captured 15 per cent of the growing draught ale market in the Republic, performing well against its principal competitors, the Guinness products Phoenix and Smithwicks, and Beamish & Crawford's Celebration.

The British seamen's strike in 1966 restricted supplies of Red Barrel from England and moves to begin brewing in Cork were given added urgency. The first brews of Red Barrel took place in the summer of 1966 and by the end of the year all the Red Barrel sold in Ireland was produced at Lady's Well Brewery. The switch to Irish production created some problems, however. The Cork-produced Red Barrel, with 'Brewed in Ireland' now printed on the label and on promotional material, met with a spate of product complaints and renewed competition from its ale competitors as well as the newly launched Harp lager on draught. Efforts to extend trade in this highly competitive market continued. Competing draught ales were gradually pushed out of Murphy's tied houses, bottled Red Barrel was introduced to the market in late 1967, and exports from Cork to Northern Ireland began.

Despite these developments, however, sales of the brand levelled off and it proved unable to break out of the narrow market segment in which it had established itself. Guinness dominated the ale market as well as the stout market. Smithwicks was the brand leader, followed by Phoenix and the smaller-selling Time, Macardles and Double Diamond. Beamish & Crawford's Celebration declined in popularity, but in 1968 its new managers Bass Charrington (who entered into an agreement with Canadian Breweries in 1967 and now controlled the Cork brewery through a subsidiary, United Breweries) began brewing Bass, which rapidly cornered 18 per cent of the draught ale market.

Stout

While ale and, to a lesser extent, lager gradually increased their share of the Irish beer market in the late 1960s, stout still accounted for approximately three-quarters of the market and was the backbone of James J. Murphy & Co. Ltd's trade and profits. However, while Red Barrel sales initially grew rapidly, sales of Murphy's Stout continued to decline.

This was a transitional period in the production of stout, with the development of the single keg system, dispensing technology and pasteurisation. Due to the delays in installing the necessary new machinery at Lady's Well, Murphy's lagged behind its competitors in the years 1965 and 1966, steadily losing trade as a result.

Continuing Decline

By the beginning of 1965 both Guinness and Beamish & Crawford had completed major schemes of reconstruction similar to that which was just beginning at Lady's Well and were now producing stout which could be served from a single cask or keg, cylindrical in shape, with the aid of a gas cylinder. The sales of this kegged stout were backed up by an unprecedented level of advertising by both companies in competition with each other, allied to extensive sponsorship of sporting and cultural events. Murphy's, in the meantime, was ahead of its competitors in the area of dispensing technology due to the ground-breaking work of Patrick Earley, but was forced to 'mark time' with its existing system until the required new machinery was installed; this inevitably led to a steady decline in trade.

In the words of the chairman, 1966 was 'a wretched year' in the brewery's stout trade. In the late spring there were problems with the flavour and condition of Murphy's Stout, and efforts at remedying the situation were impeded by major plant failures. By the time the problems were corrected towards the end of the year (Patrick Earley used the new plant to pasteurise the low stout, thus eliminating the problem of the stout going sour), much trade had been lost. Most of this was won by Guinness. Beamish & Crawford had attempted to break into the national market in that year, backed by a major advertising campaign, but succeeded only in diversifying its distribution rather than significantly increasing its sales. Its poor dispensing system was a major handicap, and the marketing drive which Guinness launched in response to its campaign resulted in that company increasing its share of the stout market. James J. Murphy & Co. Ltd and its partners decided to concentrate on the protection of its core local market against the intrusion of Guinness, and prioritise the development of its 'new stout'.

'New Stout'

The modernisation of the stout brewing side of the brewery continued while the technology was perfected by Patrick Earley, who became head brewer on 1 January 1967. He created a double tube device which allowed the dispensing of stout through one tap from a single keg. (Keg stout was brewery conditioned, as distinct from the older, less consistent and time-consuming cask conditioned product, and the use of gases did away with the need for a second cask.) The 'new stout', served through the new dispenser system with a stainless steel cover, was successfully tested in Bandon in April 1967 and installed throughout the Murphy's trading area in July, leading to a slow but steady increase in trade.

Changes in bottled stout came with the introduction of pasteurisation. Pasteurised stout in half-pint bottles was first sold on the Christmas market in 1965, and in the following year this 'new stout' was also sold in pint bottles. The initial boost in trade gave way to decline in 1967 as public taste showed a swing away from bottled beer of all makes and back to draught. This was because the keg beers gave the consistency and shelf life formerly only found in bottles, while stout advertising stressed the draught product because of the investment which had gone into the development of dispensing technology. This was the period when television beer advertising really took off and

Metal kegs, which replaced the old wooden and metal casks.

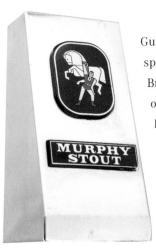

Cover for the 'new stout' dispenser.

Guinness was at the forefront, spending more on it than all the British brewers, and more than any other company of any kind in Ireland.

James J. Murphy & Co. Ltd could not hope to compete in the realm of advertising with the Dublin giant, but had to respond in some manner if its new stout was to make a mark. A television advertising campaign to promote the new Murphy's Stout began in October 1968, and this led to an upswing in sales, which had been hit by a succession of price rises throughout the year. Murphy's draught stout was sold in Dublin for the first time during this period. The rise in demand was dealt a severe blow in February and early March 1969, however, when a five week strike by maintenance and craft workers brought production at Lady's Well Brewery to a standstill. (Guinness was the only brewery which maintained production during this strike, due to a private agreement it had reached with its workers.)

Watney Mann Acquires Majority Shareholding

In the meantime, in early 1967, Watney Mann had acquired 51 per cent of the shares of James J. Murphy & Co. Ltd. Watney Mann (Ireland) Ltd, which had been based in Dublin, moved its operations to Lady's Well. The links with Watney Mann were strengthened across the board and in May 1968 Louis King became vice-chairman of Murphy's. He was succeeded as vice-chairman in November 1968 by Warren Fenwicke-Clennell of Watney Mann, who took up the new position of chief executive of James J. Murphy & Co. Ltd and of Watney Mann (Ireland) Ltd. Murphy's joint managing directors at this time were Michael Warner and Peter Dempster. The latter had been recruited by Watney's from Guinness in late 1966 and was also managing director of Watney Mann (Ireland) Ltd. Watney's had continued to invest in the Cork plant, but it was still not working to capacity while the depreciation of machinery was proving costly. It had by now invested upwards of £700,000 but was seeing little return.

'Colonel Murphy's'

Guinness domination of the Irish stout market seemed unbreakable. The building of new public houses, and improvements to its existing houses, helped Murphy's to maintain its local base, but it was realised that the development of an export trade was essential. In early 1968 Murphy's stout was test marketed in a small number of selected tied houses belonging to Wilson's Brewery, one of the Watney Mann group, in Manchester. In June 1969 a far more extensive test marketing began, as Watney Mann sought to take on Guinness in a market where brand loyalty was not as strong and advantage could be taken of the tied house system.

Watney Mann linked up with another British brewing giant, Bass Charrington, and began selling Murphy's stout through some 300 tied houses in the London and Brighton areas. The stout was brewed in Cork and was the same as that sold in Ireland, but was marketed in England, at the insistence of the advertisers there, under the name 'Colonel Murphy's'. The stout sold well and there were no complaints about either the product or the dispensers. Disaster struck in October, however, when Bass Charrington and Watney Mann made a deal with Guinness and the Colonel Murphy's experiment came to an abrupt end. The partners announced the withdrawal of the product and plans to press ahead with the immediate installation of Guinness dispensers in their 7,000 tied houses. Watney Mann chairman Peter Crossman informed Watney shareholders that 'the investment and effort required to catch up with the public awareness of draught Guinness would have been less profitable to the group than the sale of a product already successfully marketed'. Whatever the truth of the situation, and the extent to which the move made business sense in the British context, the decision was a severe blow to the Irish operation.

The Closing of the Watney Mann Era

In the same month as the collapse of the Colonel Murphy's experiment, October 1969, United Breweries (owners of Beamish & Crawford) took the historic decision to sell draught Guinness in its tied houses, in response to consumer and tenant demand. (The re-launch of Beamish stout under the name Tower had proved unsuccessful, and that brewery was now concentrating on Carling lager and Bass ale.) Murphy's regarded the United Breweries move as a serious weakening of the tied house system, the backbone of its trade, and refused its own tenants' requests to be allowed to sell Guinness. This is hardly surprising, as such a move at this stage would probably have heralded the end of Murphy's Stout. As it stood, it was sharing a mere 3 per cent of the stout market with Tower.

Red Barrel sales had continued to fall and, faced with increasing losses, Watney Mann (Ireland) Ltd reorganised and concentrated its activities in Leinster and Northern Ireland. In the second half of 1969 a number of voluntary redundancies were sought and taken, mineral bottling was transferred from Kilmallock to Bandon and there was a major re-organisation of the West Cork operation, including redundancies. These economies, however, failed to make a substantial difference. Watney Mann was experiencing difficulties in Britain also and was seeking to cut its losses. It concluded in late 1969 that further investment in Ireland could not be justified. Watney Mann informed the Murphy board in early 1970 that it was withdrawing from the trading agreement and suggested that either the company be wound up or another trading partner be found. (A new ale called Anvil was test marketed by Murphy's in Cork with little success, due mainly to lack of funds for marketing.)

From March until late summer 1970 unsuccessful efforts were made to find a new trading partner. In the absence of expected government assistance to save the company in the interests of maintaining employment, Watney Mann decided in October 1970 that, in order to protect the assets of the company and put further pressure on the government, it would file a winding up petition by demanding the repayment of loans it had made to James J. Murphy & Co. Ltd. The High Court dismissed the petition in November, and in January 1971 Watney Mann agreed to withhold any further action to wind up the company until the government had made a decision.

Despite intensive lobbying, the government

took no action and by April 1971 it appeared that the Murphy's story had come to an end. Liquidation moves had begun and redundancy notices were being prepared when, at the 'eleventh hour', the Fianna Fáil government under Jack Lynch, in whose constituency the brewery was located, intervened. Negotiations began between Watney Mann and the state rescue agency Taiscí Stáit Teoranta (TST), which operated under the control of the Industrial Credit Company. On 8 June 1971 an agreement was signed by Watney Mann, TST and James J. Murphy & Co. Ltd.

New Board

According to the terms of the agreement, Watney Mann Ltd accepted £420,000 in full settlement of its investment in the brewery, which was in the region of £700,000. The money was lent by TST to James J. Murphy & Co. Ltd, who paid it over immediately. Watney Mann also sold its 51 per cent shareholding (worth £520,000) to TST for £100,000. The trading agreement between the two companies was terminated and the brewing and sale of Red Barrel in Ireland ceased. TST required that the Murphy board be reduced in size, that it should nominate four of the directors including the chairman, and that a chief executive or managing director should be recruited as soon as possible.

To meet with the requirements for a reduced board, Patrick Earley, head brewer, T. O'Higgins, secretary, and J. G. Scroope, personnel and wine and spirits division manager, were asked to resign from the board, though they remained in executive control of their departments. The TST nominees (chairman Eddie Power, Aidan Murray, William O'Brien and Tom Higgins)

joined the Colonel on the new board, whose first task was the selection of a managing director. William F. (Bill) O'Connell, a Corkman who was marketing director at a fertilizer firm in County Wexford was chosen and he took up his appointment on 1 January 1972.

Turning the Corner

The first major development of the new era was the signing of an agreement with Irish Ale Breweries to handle Smithwicks. The ale, which was the brand leader, was delivered in tank from the Kilkenny brewery, pumped into the cold room at Lady's Well, racked, kegged and sold

The board of James J. Murphy & Co. Ltd, 1972-1974.
Back row, left to right: William O'Brien, Aidan Murray and Tom Higgins;
front row, left to right: Lt Col John F. Murphy, Eddie Power (chairman), and Bill O'Connell (managing director).

through Murphy's tied houses. The company also began storing wheat and barley, and malting on commission, for the Malting Company of Ireland. The 'cash and carry' turnover showed a considerable improvement and the West Cork Bottling Co. began operating at full capacity.

Trading losses for the year ending 30 June 1972 were reduced to £32,000 as against £45,000 for the previous trading year. The renovation of tied houses continued, as did the racking of Smithwicks for the tied trade and general distribution in West Cork. This operation was not very profitable, but was considered important as it helped to maintain operations and keep up staff morale. For the first time in many years there was an increase in stout sales. This was achieved with the help of newspaper advertising and the sponsorship of a number of local events, most notably a high profile soccer match between German star team Borussia Mönchengladbach and a 'Murphy Munster Stars' selection. This event played a major part in putting the Murphy name back before the Cork public. Stout sales continued to show a slow but steady increase over the next two years. At the time of the TST rescue, Murphy's Stout sales were at an all time low of approximately 11,000 barrels per annum. By September 1972 sales had risen to 14,472 barrels, and a year later stood at 14, 879.

The company's subsidiaries, the West Cork Bottling Company and W. H. O'Sullivan and Sons of Kilmallock, also turned the corner, and both managed to turn substantial losses into small trading profits. In 1972 the company negotiated with Batchelors the sole agency for the distribution of Canada Dry products in Munster,

A Murphy's float on Patrick's Street, Cork, in the 1960s.

and also became the sole Munster agents for the mineral range of Savage Smyth of Dublin, the largest wholesale bottlers in the country.

Whitbread Trophy

Despite these positive developments, there remained the fundamental problem of the costly under-utilisation of the brewing plant which had been developed in the late 1960s. The company did not possess the resources to launch a beer of its own and a major priority was the securing of a franchise for the brewing of an existing brand. Approaches were made to continental and British brewers, and the end result was an agreement in 1973 with Whitbread, the third largest brewing group in Britain at the time. It was agreed that James J. Murphy & Co. Ltd would brew Whitbread's Trophy draught ale under licence for the Irish market. Trophy was the third largest selling beer in Britain, and after extensive studies of the Irish beer market, it was adapted to suit Irish requirements. Trophy was successfully launched and was well received. The company, however, lacked the resources to sustain the marketing effort necessary to establish Trophy as a profitable brand and it was withdrawn from the market in 1974.

The Licensed Vintners Co-operative Society

In early 1974 the outlook for James J. Murphy & Co. Ltd was bleak. No dividend had been paid to shareholders since 1969 and, with annual sales of under 15,000 barrels in an increasingly competitive and expensive market, losses were growing. These losses grew from £32,000 in 1972 to £223,000 in 1973. In spite of these difficulties, a group called Pembroke Investments made a bid for the company. Fóir Teoranta and the directors of Murphy's were favourable to Pembroke Investments' approach, but an improved offer was made by another interest.

P. J. Meagher is regarded as having been the catalyst in the new bid. He knew the brewing industry and was an experienced management consultant. He brought together a group of publicans (or vintners) and the Licensed Vintners Co-operative Society was established. The licensed trade was invited to subscribe for shares issued on behalf of this society to fund the acquisition of James J. Murphy & Co. Ltd. The appeal was well received and over 1,000 vintners subscribed. The 48.7 per cent of the brewery equity not held by Fóir Teoranta was purchased with its agreement in April 1974. The vintners' group also declared its intention to eventually purchase the remaining 51.3 per cent of the company's equity.

With the agreement of Fóir Teoranta, still the majority shareholder, a new board was put in place to direct the affairs of the brewery. The connection with the Murphy family was maintained with the appointment of Lt. Col. J. F. Murphy as Honorary Life President. The new chairman was W. J. (Bill) McDonogh and Michael Long was appointed Managing Director in place

of Bill O'Connell who had managed the brewery over two of its most difficult years. The other executive directors were Patrick Early, head brewer, P. J. Meagher, who had charge of sales and marketing, and J. W. Regan, financial controller.

Objectives

The stated principal objective of the new management team was to ensure viable competition in the drinks trade. Guinness controlled over 90 per cent of the market and many vintners were fearful of the consequences if Murphy's, the last independent Irish brewery, were to close. With competition between suppliers it was felt that favourable credit terms and the supply and service, without charge, of dispensers, cooling equipment and other point of sale material would continue to be a feature of the trade in Ireland.

The board of LVH, the holding company of James J. Murphy and Co. Ltd: Standing (l-r): Aidan Murray and Willie O'Brien (Fóir Teo), Jack O'Connor (Murphy Vintners' Association), Paddy McKiernan and Kevin Delaney, (LV Co-operative Society) Seated (l-r): Mick Walsh (LV Co-operative Society) Bill McDonogh, (Chairman) and Eddie Power (Fóir Teo).

Another aim was to provide a total drinks service to the trade. This would necessitate the establishment of an ale and lager in addition to Murphy's Stout, as well as supplying bottled beers, soft drinks, wines and spirits, supported by wholesaling and cash-and-carry operations where appropriate. The planned expansion and diversification would be expensive and a turn-around in the fortunes of Murphy's Stout, the brewery's principal product, was regarded as essential to fund the developments. The new board also wished to free the many brewery tenants of their tie and to sell the brewery's 150 or so tied public houses. In essence, it was felt that success was assured because the new shareholders, mostly publicans, would also be the retailers of their company's products.

Initial Success

The change in ownership of the brewery coincided with an industrial dispute at Guinness in Dublin. Supplies of Guinness were severely restricted and Lady's Well Brewery worked at full capacity to supply Murphy's Stout to the licensed trade. Much of the extra production was directed to the Dublin market, where Murphy's hoped to gain a solid foothold. This, coupled with a new optimism generated by the management team, increased sales of Murphy's dramatically. Sales of 14,879 barrels in the year ended September 1973 jumped to 30,423 barrels by the end of September 1974. Most of this increase occurred in the months after April and a sizeable proportion was accounted for in the Dublin area. Turnover grew to over £3.7 million and though a loss of £289,000 was recorded, the indications were positive for the future.

Over the following three years or so the brewery performed well. Sales grew to 59,759 barrels in 1975 and profits grew to £108,000. By 1976 sales had increased to 94,263 barrels and profits grew corres-pondingly to £430,000 nett. Draught Murphy, the company's major product, had ten per cent of the (albeit shrinking) Irish stout market by 1976 and output at the brewery was reaching levels not achieved since the early years of the century. Draught stout was now being dis-tributed throughout the southern counties and also in Dublin and in the west of Ireland. The slogan 'Join the Murphy Movement' was coined to promote the product and in 1977 new television commercials were launched and marketing and promotional activity was intensified. One of the new commercials, 'The Murphy Saunter', won an Irish advertising industry award. In 1979 the continuing success of Murphy's Stout in Ireland

Heineken Market Share Still Growing.
Canada Dry Soft Drinks Launched.
New W&S Company Announced - see
Special Wine & Spirit Supplement
Six Picture Pages from Around the Trade

MURPHY EXPORTS TO UNITED STATES

Export Murphy at Big U.S. Beer Convention

The first containerload of bottled Murphy sailed from Cork to New York on Thursday 18 November, and Murphy will be heavily featured at the US Beer Distributors National Convention in Florida towards the end of this month. The Stateside export Murphy is repackaged in a new export carton plus new designs for carrypacks, bottles and labels.

prompted exports, on an experimental basis, to the UK, the US and Canada.

The company's wholesaling activities were rationalised. Depots were now functioning in Cork city and in the county towns of Bandon and Skibbereen, in Dublin, and in Kilmallock, County Limerick. The range of products offered to customers at these 'one stop shops' was expanded. Leading brands of spirits were stocked and the company established exclusive agencies for other brands of imported spirits and wines. In 1976 the company launched its own brands of vodka and gin, distilled in Ireland. These were sold under the names of Zamirov and Tolstoy vodka and Shandon and Holloways gin. Bottled beers were also supplied, along with fruit cordials and soft drinks under the Spring brand, produced by the West Cork Bottling Co. in Bandon. The wines and spirits division was a consistently good performer and traded profitably. In 1979 a new wholly owned subsidiary, Murphy's Brewery Wines and Spirits Ltd, was set up by the brewery. It was managed by Bob Kennefick and had its headquarters in Dublin.

Tied Houses

In keeping with its objectives, the new board began the process of selling off the brewery's estate of tied public houses. Publicans had long believed the tied house system to be unfair, restrictive and outdated and repeatedly campaigned for its abolition, but breweries with tied estates always resisted moves to break the tie. Circumstances were now somewhat changed, however, as vintners were major shareholders in the company. The new attitude was that the trade in general would be better off with free trading.

The cost of maintaining and decorating tied houses had always been borne by the brewery and this had now grown to be a substantial annual charge, while the rents paid by tenants were in many cases non-commercial. The sale of the tied houses would not only remove these difficulties, but would also generate substantial income which could be used to finance proposed developments.

In 1974 £75,037 in profit was generated by the sale of tied houses and in the following year further sales brought in an additional £163,608. The surviving houses, almost 100 in all, were valued at over £600,000. A mortgage scheme was introduced for tenants to ease the further disposal of the assets, but the take-up on the offer slowed somewhat from 1977. Sales continued, however, and the majority of the houses were sold over the following years.

New Ales

In the early 1970s the Irish ale market was an expanding sector. In 1967 ale accounted for 15 per cent of Irish beer sales; by 1975 this had grown to 31 per cent. Over the same period stout's share of the total market had fallen from 80 per cent to 58 per cent. It was regarded as essential to have an ale in the brewery's portfolio. Earlier experiments with Anvil and Trophy were shortlived, and the new management was eager to establish a successful ale. Schooner ale was developed by the Murphy's brewing team under the direction of Patrick Earley. It was test-marketed during 1975 and was released to the trade in December of that year. A television commercial was shot in England using the *Charlotte Rhodes*, a schooner which figured prominently in *The Onedin Line*, a very popular

The natural bite and body of success

YOUNGER'S ALE

Younger's, part of Scotland's tradition for great drink, is already a firm favourite with Irish ale drinkers.

Younger's the fastest growing ale in Ireland today.

television series of the time. In spite of the commercial and a wide distribution, Schooner had a relatively low profile and in 1977 plans were advanced to put weighty advertising support behind the ale for the summer months.

The plans to re-launch Schooner were abandoned, however, when consumer research indicated that Scottish and Newcastle's Youngers ale, which Murphy's had been considering as an alternative, would prove more attractive to Irish ale drinkers. Brewing facilities were expanded to facilitate the production of Youngers in Cork and it was launched on the Irish market in the summer of 1977. In spite of a large expenditure on marketing and advertising, Youngers did not perform to expectations in the highly competitive ale sector. In 1979 it was re-launched in Dublin and Galway as Youngers Tartan Special, but never succeeded in winning and holding a large enough share of the market.

Heineken

In 1975 Murphy's brewery made its first efforts at securing the right to brew Heineken under licence in Cork. The Murphy's chairman, in his review of that year, remarked: 'We feel there is an interesting future for Heineken lager.' Whitbread was, at that time, brewing Heineken in the United Kingdom and it was test-marketed in a number of pubs in Dublin between December 1974 and June 1975. It was felt that a stronger version of Heineken would be needed to compete in the growing lager market in Ireland. Whitbread chose not to invest in James J. Murphy

& Co. Ltd and Murphy's made a direct approach to Heineken N.V. with a view to starting a licenced operation in Ireland.

The potential of the Cork brewery was assessed by Heineken. Murphy's financial position was considered weak, but Schooner ale still looked promising at that time and had the potential to become quite profitable. The brewery's location in Cork was considered possibly problematic from a distribution point of view as over 40 per cent of national lager consumption was in the Dublin area. Murphy's brewing facilities would need upgrading to Heineken standards but the stronger Heineken, more suited to Irish tastes, could be imported from Holland for test purposes while the upgrading was underway. One of the principal factors which swayed the Dutch company to accept the Murphy approach was the support that Murphy's brewery enjoyed among publicans, who wished to see meaningful competition between suppliers. In addition, the Irish lager market was growing and an early positioning in the marketplace would be an important advantage.

A licence agreement was signed and a marketing company, Heineken Ireland, was set up as a wholly-owned subsidiary of Heineken N.V. The price, packaging, marketing, advertising and positioning of the lager would be under Heineken control and an agreement was also made whereby Heineken had responsibility for the brewing of its product. The association with Heineken, though not without its difficulties in the years prior to

1982, proved to be a link that eventually led to the rescue of Murphy's and the survival of the brewery.

Bottling Plant

While negotiations were underway with Heineken it was decided that a larger and more up-to-date bottling plant would be desirable for bottling the new lager. It was also planned to centralise all bottling activity (for beers, soft drinks, juices and cordials) at the new plant. Up to then bottling had taken place in Cork, Bandon and Kilmallock. In August 1976 a site on the Kinsale Road on the outskirts of the city was purchased for £150,000 and work on the construction of the new bottling plant began.

In 1976 the brewery management was confident and bullish. Profits had risen to over £400,000 on a turnover of over £10 million. Murphy's Stout had 10 per cent of the Irish stout market and in all its various spheres of activity the brewery was performing well. The continuing re-equipment and expansion of the brewery's interests required increased capital. As there were limitations on the individual shareholdings in a co-operative society (the nature of the vintners holding company), it was decided to convert to a public company. The remaining shares in James J. Murphy & Co. Ltd held by Fóir Teoranta were purchased and Murphy's Brewery Limited came into being. The sum of £650,000 in additional share capital was issued and the optimism of investors was reflected in the fact that the offer was oversubscribed.

The optimism of 1976 led to ambitious plans for the new bottling plant, which was to be equipped to produce 20,000 units per hour. It was planned that stout, ale, lager, soft drinks and juices would be bottled in a variety of capacities. During the following year, however, circumstances changed and a combination of external and internal factors led to difficulties that were never surmounted and contributed to losses that severely damaged the company's well-being.

The commissioning of the bottling line was delayed until October 1978 and even then it was beset by technical difficulties. It was not possible to efficiently bottle a broad range of products in the variety of capacities required. The company acquired the franchise for the production of Canada Dry soft drinks, mixers and juices and hoped that this would be a profitable area of development. Canada Dry was an attractive brand and during 1979 the Spring range of soft drinks was converted to the new label. In the latter part of 1979, however, it was still proving difficult to optimise the operation of the plant. This resulted in stock shortages during the crucial Christmas period, and the demands of the trade could not be met.

The problems associated with the bottling plant led to a certain level of disunity on the board. Though it reached target production levels on soft drinks in 1980, the overall projections for the plant were never met. By the end of 1980 it had cost the company in the region of £3 million in capital expenditure and operating losses. These costs could not be carried and eclipsed the profitable operation of the other sectors of the company's business. In an effort to stem these losses the plant was offered for sale in 1981 as part of a restructuring plan.

Difficulties

During the first three years or so of the vintners' stewardship the brewery prospered. Losses were turned into respectable profits, dividends were paid to shareholders, sales and turnover grew and there was investment in all areas of the company's business. The 1976 share offer was oversubscribed and the experiment of a section of the licensed trade operating a brewery was deemed to be a success. By 1977, however, optimism was being dented a little. Profits were down on increased turnover to about half the 1976 level and borrowings increased by £850,000. At this time price increases had to be cleared by the National Prices Commission and an increase granted in January 1977 was not passed on to the consumer by the breweries until nine months later. Guinness had decided on this

Aerial view of the brewery in the mid-1970s.

course of action and the much smaller Cork brewery felt it would be unwise to raise its prices above those of its principal rival. This, coupled with higher duties, made trading conditions difficult. There were further difficulties in the following year. In July 1978 tougher drink–driving legislation came into force and the upward trend in the beer market noted in the

first half of the year was halted. Heineken was launched in April 1978, and though it performed extremely well in winning a 9 per cent share of the draught lager market in its first year, considerable expenditure was necessary on new brewing facilities. The delays in the commissioning of the new bottling plant also entailed extra spending, resulting in increased borrowing. Overall, the company's trading profit dropped to £12,000, compared to over £200,000 in the previous twelve months. The planned funding of developments at the brewery with the profits from stout sales never occurred.

General economic conditions in Ireland at this time added to the difficulties that the company was experiencing. Credit was tight, interest rates were high and, with high inflation, costs were increasingly difficult to control. The brewery developed serious cash-flow problems and Heineken N.V. was approached and asked for the first time to take a direct interest in the company. The request was turned down on the basis that the sales projections for 1979 were overly optimistic and that Heineken was more interested in the development of the Heineken brand in Ireland, rather than in the total development of Murphy's Brewery and its various divisions.

In spite of the adverse conditions Murphy's Brewery Ltd showed a trading profit of £244,000 for 1979 on a turnover of £19 million. This figure, however, was not regarded as a sufficient return on the capital invested in the business. While Murphy's Stout, Heineken and the wines and spirits division did well, the losses on the bottling plant, the costs incurred in improving brewing facilities, and high interest rates on borrowings made the overall picture rather bleak.

Trying to Survive

In 1980 attempts were made to consolidate. As the chairman Bill McDonogh noted: 'We have instituted a far-reaching programme of serious cost reduction ... designed to effect every possible and sensible saving in every single sector of the Company's operations'. Heineken lager was to be the exception and would be supported by heavy marketing expenditure. However, increased demand for Heineken would necessitate an expansion of brewing capacity and a consequent need for increased capital. In May 1980 the Murphy's board requested a £600,000 contribution from Heineken N.V., preferably in the form of redeemable preference shares, to enable the expansion of Heineken brewing capacity in Cork. The request was turned down as Heineken felt that such an investment would be of only short-term benefit. Instead, a joint Murphy's-Heineken working party was set up to examine Murphy's long-term viability.

The working group reported in November 1980 and noted that past profit performance was very unsatisfactory in terms of return on capital.

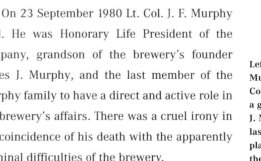

In spite of this the group felt that Murphy's Stout could retake 7.5 per cent of the stout market within three years (it had fallen to below 5 per cent) and that Youngers Tartan Special ale could capture 5 per cent of the ale market by 1985. This growth would, of course, be dependent on increased and more frequent marketing expenditure. Heineken was thought capable of an 11 per cent share of the lager market by 1985 and up to 20 per cent by 1988. However, these growth figures would require increased distribution and marketing costs in addition to investment to increase brewing capacity. The working party estimated the costs of these developments at £10.8 million between then and 1988. Profits, before interest, depreciation and other write-offs, were projected to rise to £5.7 million by 1988. It was recommended that Heineken take a share of at least 20 per cent in Murphy's. This was rejected by Heineken's corporate staff. Sales projections were felt to be overly optimistic and the financial return was regarded as too low. There were some reservations also about the strength of Murphy's management.

During 1980 the financial position of Murphy's Brewery Limited deteriorated further. Losses grew to over £600,000 and borrowings grew to over £4 million. Bill McDonogh, chairman, remarked in his annual review of the year that he found himself 'faced with reporting the worst financial results since the Brewery was bought by the Vintners in 1974'. He felt that the company, since 1974, had expanded too rapidly to achieve its objectives. Having invested heavily in expansion, the difficult trading conditions of later years had seen resources spread too thinly and activities spread too widely.

On 23 September 1980 Lt. Col. J. F. Murphy died. He was Honorary Life President of the company, grandson of the brewery's founder James J. Murphy, and the last member of the Murphy family to have a direct and active role in the brewery's affairs. There was a cruel irony in the coincidence of his death with the apparently terminal difficulties of the brewery.

Bill McDonogh, company chairman, 1974-1982.

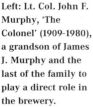

Left: Lt. Col. John F. Murphy, 'The Colonel' (1909-1980), a grandson of James J. Murphy and the last of the family to play a direct role in the brewery.

10

Murphy Brewery Ireland Limited

1983 -

Heineken sent J. J. Cronin, a native of County Cork, from headquarters to act as general manager of Murphy Brewery Ireland Limited and oversee the beginning of a new era. A long-term plan was developed for the transformation of the brewery, its products and its fortunes.

Transforming Lady's Well Brewery

A fundamental initial requirement was the transformation of the antiquated brewery which Heineken had acquired into one equipped for the demands of the modern marketplace, in Ireland and abroad. A huge investment programme was undertaken to modernise and expand the facilities at Lady's Well, and what was essentially a new brewery was built on the site of the old plant. By 1985 £10 million had been spent on building a new brewhouse and kegging plant, and on improving yeast storage and treatment, water treatment and malt handling facilities. The old brewhouse was demolished and the 199 foot Murphy's chimney stack, for so long a well known landmark and

The old 199 foot chimney stack at Lady's Well Brewery, a famous Cork landmark, demolished for safety reasons in 1985.

Left: The old malt house, converted into the modern headquarters of Murphy Brewery Ireland Ltd, opened in 1992.

feature of the Cork skyline, also came down in 1985. The old Lady's Well malt house was preserved, however, and transformed into an award-winning modern office building, the new headquarters of Murphy Brewery Ireland Ltd. which was officially opened in 1992. By 1988 over £20 million had been invested in the brewery, and by the mid-1990s Heineken had spent over £55 million in upgrading its Irish subsidiary.

Other Changes

As well as transforming the brewery itself, the new management set about remodelling the entire company. Reorganisation saw the workforce of 220 cut by around fifty through a combination of early retirement and voluntary redundancies, while new work practices, such as requiring all employees and managers to clock in, were introduced. (By the mid-1990s the company employed over 380 people.) Retraining programmes for old employees and training for new recruits was provided with financial support from the Industrial Development Authority. National distribution of the brewery's products was made more efficient, and a Draught Beer Service Organisation ensured that beer installations were clean and operating properly.

In 1984 the Heineken management team at Murphy's drew up elaborate marketing plans which had the overall objective of reviving Murphy's Stout and increasing Heineken's presence in the lager market.

141

Murphy's Irish Stout

In the early 1980s Murphy's Stout was basically a regional brand, little known outside Cork and other parts of Munster. The immediate priority was to consolidate the Munster base, after which distribution would be expanded nationally and

internationally. The management felt that the brand could become a credible contender in a market dominated by Guinness.

A number of steps were taken towards the revival of the brand. The quality of the product was improved and adapted in line with the results of consumer tests. A new livery was designed and the stout was renamed Murphy's Irish Stout. The marketing strategy for the stout pushed the message that this was a different product to Guinness, 'a different story': Murphy's was a smoother, premium stout for the discerning drinker. While a declining stout market (nationally and internationally) and the danger of an aggressive reaction from Guinness were seen as threats to the success of Murphy's Irish Stout, a number of key factors were identified which would help its expansion. In Ireland the goodwill of the Vintners' Association, which had feared a Guinness monopoly, was crucial and this resistance to monopoly was replicated in the trade internationally. The

support of Heineken, the world's second largest brewer in terms of volume and the leading international brewer in terms of geographical spread, was a major plus, while the fact that Murphy's was an authentic Irish brand with an identifiably Irish name was also an advantage.

The launch of Murphy's Irish Stout as a national and international brand took place in November 1985. The new livery was introduced as was a new 25cl long neck bottle, unique in the stout market. An advertising campaign with the theme of 'Murphy's Irish Stout: Tradition in the Making' spearheaded the marketing drive which would see the brand distributed throughout Ireland and exported first to the UK and subsequently across the world. It was announced that Murphy's Irish Stout was now one of Heineken's three corporate brands, along with Heineken and Amstel lagers.

Murphy's in the UK

The UK was the largest stout market in the world and it was here, in 1985, that Murphy's Irish Stout first became available outside Ireland. It was brewed in the UK under licence by Whitbread, a long term partner of Heineken's. National distribution began in the UK in 1988 and by the mid-1990s Murphy's Irish Stout had won 15 per cent of the stout market there. In August 1991 Whitbread launched draught Murphy's in a can, using the unique Draughtflow system. This proved highly successful in the growing take-home stout market, and was launched in Ireland in October 1992.

Expanding Murphy's Exports

Using the experience of the UK market as a reference, Murphy Brewery began exporting stout to other parts of the world in the late 1980s. Exports began to continental Europe, with particular attention being paid to the speciality beer markets in Germany and France. With the aid of Heineken's distribution network the brand had access to over 150 countries worldwide, and the number of those countries importing Murphy's Irish Stout grew annually. By the mid-1990s the Cork stout was available in over sixty countries. Among the factors which contributed to the international success of Murphy's Irish Stout were its accessible taste, its rich heritage, the fact that it is a genuine Irish product and the growth of the Irish pub phenomenon. In the UK in 1995 Whitbread opened the first of a series of Irish themed bars under the banner 'J. J. Murphy & Co.', and in the same year the first of the Murphy's Irish pubs on the continent of Europe, 'The Irish Rover' in Madrid, was opened. Subsequently Heineken, Murphy Brewery and the Specialist Joinery Group came together in a joint venture, Murphy's Pubs of Ireland. This initiative made it possible to have a genuine Irish traditional pub created anywhere in the world.

Heineken Lager

The second major objective of the new management team at Murphy Brewery was to increase Heineken's presence in the increasingly competitive lager market in Ireland, and in this they matched the success achieved with Murphy's Irish Stout.

Guinness, which had six draught lagers in its portfolio, led the market with Harp. However, Heineken, backed by an innovative marketing

J.J. Cronin, 1983.

Gerry van Soest, 1984-1988.

Frans van der Milne, 1988-1989.

Michael Foley, 1989-1993.

Marien Kakebeeke, 1993-

Left: Murphy's in the USA: outside the Rockefeller Center, New York.

campaign, became the fastest growing lager and in 1989 became the first beer to overtake a Guinness brand in Ireland when it supplanted Harp as the market leader. It subsequently consolidated its position as Ireland's most popular lager and by 1996 its market share was a full seventeen percentage points ahead of its nearest rivals at 39 per cent.

Other Brands

Despite being the fastest growing lager in the late 1980s, the increasingly fierce competition in the sector was seen as threatening because it was the company's only lager brand in Ireland. In 1988 a decision was made to launch a second lager, Amstel, as a so-called 'heat shield' to prevent Heineken being undercut in price. Though Amstel was the number two lager in Holland, number one in Greece and very popular in many other countries it failed to make an impact in Ireland and was withdrawn in late 1989. In 1996, however, Amstel made a return to Ireland when it was re-launched in canned form.

In 1988 Murphy Brewery entered the then growing low-alcohol beer sector with the launch

of Buckler, brewed by Heineken. It quickly became the number two brand in the market, and maintained this position and increased its share despite the overall decline in popularity of low alcohol beers.

In 1993 Murphy entered the premium bottled speciality lager market with the launch of Coors Extra Gold, an American lager aimed at younger drinkers. It performed well and in 1995 the brewery launched bottled Coors Light.

Sponsorship

The success of Murphy Brewery products was helped by a number of high profile sponsorships. In November 1993 the brewery announced its sponsorship of the annual Irish Open Golf Championship. The first Murphy's Irish Open was staged in 1994 and was the most successful golfing championship ever staged in Ireland. This sponsorship played a major part in enhancing the image of Murphy's Irish Stout nationally and internationally. In the UK, the brand sponsored the Murphy's English Open Golf Championship; other Murphy's sponsorships included the Cork Film Festival, the Murphy's Cat Laughs international comedy festival in Kilkenny, the Clarinbridge Oyster Festival, the National Hunt Festival at Punchestown and a range of other national and local sporting and cultural events.

Heineken sponsored many major international events, such as the Rugby World Cup in 1995. At a national level Heineken was prominent as a major supporter of music events, fashion, sailing, tennis and showjumping. Buckler sponsored car rallying and athletics, while Coors was associated with American-related pursuits in Ireland such as the American Softball League.

MURPHY'S
IRISH
OPEN
AT DRUIDS GLEN

Continued Expansion and Growth

By the mid-1990s Murphy Brewery Ireland Limited was firmly established as the second force in the Irish beer market, with sales of its brands reaching record levels. The company increased its overall share of the Irish beer market to 16.3 per cent in 1996. This growth was helped by the launch in March 1995 of Murphy's Irish Stout Draught in a bottle, a revolutionary development in the beer market. Murphy's continued to grow in the UK, where 1.5 million pints of Murphy's were being consumed each week a decade after it was first launched there. Worldwide exports continued to grow with increased sales in the US, Europe and in the southern hemisphere, particularly in the Gulf States and Australia. In November 1995 the company signed an agreement with Dominion Breweries in New Zealand to brew the Cork brewery's products under licence.

In January 1995 a new product, Murphy's Irish Red Beer was launched on the international market. (The same product was launched on the US market in 1996 under the name Murphy's

Right: 'J.J. Murphy & Co.' pub, Chelsea, London.

Irish Amber). Murphy's Red compliments Murphy's Irish Stout and strengthens Murphy's brand presence across the world. This has been further supported by the international growth of the Irish pub phenomenon and more especially of the Murphy's Pubs of Ireland concept.

The brewing of Murphy's Irish Red/Amber, albeit for the export market only, has seen Lady's Well Brewery come full circle since 1856 when James J. Murphy & Co. first brewed Lady's Well Ale along with Murphy's Porter. The brewery has survived on its original Cork site, and though its demise seemed imminent in 1971 and again in 1982, the Murphy name and tradition live on and the Murphy's story continues to unfold. ▌

BIBLIOGRAPHY

Books and Articles

Anon., 'A Book-Loving Irish Bishop', *The Irish Book Lover*, Vol. 2, 1910.

Anon., 'Catholic Parish Churches of Cork: SS. Peter and Paul's', *Journal of the Cork Historical and Archaeological Society*, Vol. 48, 1943.

Anon., 'Cork Savings Bank - 1817-1917', *Journal of the Cork Historical and Archaeological Society*, Vol. 23, 1917.

Anon., 'Great Irish Book Collectors: 1. Bishop John Murphy', *The Irish Book Lover*, Vol. 7, 1915.

Anon., 'New Offices at Lady's Well Brewery, Cork', *The Irish Builder*, Vol. 35, 1893.

Anon., *A Day at Lady's Well Brewery*, Cork, 1902.

Anon., *Burke's Irish Family Records*, London, 1976.

Anon., 'Holy Wells', *Journal of the Cork Historical and Archaeological Society*, Vol. 51, 1946.

Anon., *Rebel Cork's Fighting Story: From 1916 to the Truce with Britain*, Tralee, 1947.

Anon., *The First Sixty Years: Ford in Ireland 1917-1977*, Cork, 1977.

Anon., *The West Cork Bottling Company Limited: 100 Years 1896-1995*.

Barnard, Alfred, *The Noted Breweries of Great Britain and Ireland*, Vols 1-4, London, 1889-1891.

Beecher, Seán, *A Miscellany of Cork History*, Cork, 1992.

Bielenberg, Andy, 'The Irish Brewing Industry and the Rise of Guinness' in R. Wilson and T. Gourvish, *The Modern Brewing Industry*, London, 1997.

Bielenberg, Andy, *Cork's Industrial Revolution 1780-1880: Development or Decline?*, Cork, 1991.

Booth, John, *A Toast to Ireland: A Celebration of Traditional Irish Drinks*, Belfast, 1995.

Bowman, Marcus, 'The Brewing Industry in the Republic of Ireland', unpublished M. Econ. Soc. thesis, UCC, 1983.

Browne, Terence, Ireland: *A Social and Cultural History, 1922-1985*, London, 1985.

Buckley, James, 'Bishop Murphy: The Man and His Books', *The Irish Book Lover*, Vol. 3, 1912.

Carroll, John, 'Murphy's War', *Success*, November 1985.

Carroll, Joseph T., *Ireland in the War Years 1939-1945*, Newton Abbot, 1975.

Coakley, D.J. (ed.), *Cork: Its Trade and Commerce*, Cork, 1919.

Coleman, J. C., 'The Craft of Coopering', *Journal of the Cork Historical and Archaeological Society*, Vol. 49, 1944.

Conlon, M.V., 'Some Old Cork Charities', *Journal of the Cork Historical and Archaeological Society*, Vol. 47, 1942.

Coonan, Clifford, 'Murphy Tackles Uncle', *Business and Finance*, 23 June 1994.

Corr, Frank, 'The many trials of competing with Guinness', *Business and Finance*, 17 April, 1970.

Corran, H.S., *A History of Brewing*, Newton Abbot, 1975.

Cosgrave, Michael B., 'A History of Beamish and Crawford', unpublished MA thesis, UCC, 1989.

Coyne, William P., *Ireland, Industrial and Agricultural*, Dublin, 1902.

Cullen, L.M., *An Economic History of Ireland Since 1600*, (second edition), London, 1987.

Cummins, N. Marshall, *Some Chapters of Cork Medical History*, Cork, 1957.

Daly, Mary E., *The Social and Economic History of Ireland Since 1800*, Dublin, 1981.

Daly, Seán, *Cork: A City in Crisis - A History of Labour Conflict and Social Misery 1870-1872*, Vol. 1, Cork, 1978.

Daniel, T.K., 'Griffith on his Noble Head: The Determinants of Cumann na nGaedheal Economic Policy, 1922-32', *Irish Economic and Social History*, Vol.3, 1976.

Dickson, D. 'An Economic History of the Cork Region in the Eighteenth Century', unpublished PhD thesis, UCD, 1977.

Donnelly, James S., *The Land and People of Nineteenth Century Cork: The Rural Economic and Land Question*, London and Boston, 1975.

Dunne, Jim, 'The Struggle for Murphys', *Business and Finance*, 17 December 1981.

Fitzgerald, John, *Legends, Ballads and Songs of the Lee*, Cork, 1913.

Fitzgibbon, Frank, 'Going Dutch at Murphy's', *Business and Finance*, 1 September 1983.

Fitzpatrick, David (ed.), *Ireland and the First World War*, Dublin, 1988.

Fitzpatrick, David, 'Strikes in Ireland, 1914-1921', *Saothar*, No. 6, 1980.

Gourvish, T. R. and G. Wilson, *The British Brewing Industry 1830-1980*, Cambridge, 1994.

Hall, F. G., *The Bank of Ireland 1783-1946*, Dublin and Oxford, 1949.

Hawkins, K. and C. Pass, *The Brewing Industry*, London, 1979.

Joyce, Carmel, 'Bottoms Up at Murphys', *Business and Finance*, 10 June 1993.

Kelly, Mick and Eddie O'Gorman, 'Murphy's on the Road Again', *Vintners' World*, July 1983.

Keogh, Dermot, *Twentieth Century Ireland: Nation and State*, Dublin, 1994.

Lahiff, Edward, 'Industry and Labour in Cork, 1890-1921', unpublished MA thesis, UCC, 1988.

Lee, J. J., *Ireland 1912-1985: Politics and Society*, Cambridge, 1989.

Luke, Gerald, 'Rewriting Murphy's Law', *Business and Finance*, 20 June 1991.

Lynch, Patrick and John Vaizey, *Guinness's Brewery in the Irish Economy, 1759-1876*, Cambridge, 1960.

Mac Carthy, B. G., 'Black Eagle of The North: The Story of Archdeacon John Murphy', *Studies*, Vol. 38, 1949.

Mac Lysaght, Edward, *Irish Families: Their Names, Arms and Origins*, Dublin, 1957.

Malcolm, Elizabeth, *Ireland Sober, Ireland Free*, Dublin, 1986.

Malone, Andrew, 'A Great Irish Industry: Messrs. Arthur Guinness, Son and Co. Ltd.', *Studies*, Vols. 15 and 16, 1926-7.

Manning, Maurice and Moore McDowell, *Electricity Supply in Ireland: The History of the ESB*, Dublin, 1984.

McCarthy, Eoin and Gerard O'Sullivan, 'Recruiting and Recruits in County Cork during the First World War, 1914-1918', *Times Past - Journal of the Ballincollig Community School Local History Society*, Vol. 7, 1990-91.

Murphy, Maura, 'Cork Commercial Society 1850-1899: Politics and Problems', in P. Butel and L. M. Cullen (eds), *Cities and Merchants: French and Irish Perspectives on Urban Development, 1500-1900*, Dublin, 1986.

Murphy, Maura, 'The Economic and Social Structure of Nineteenth Century Cork', in David Harkness and Mary O'Dowd (eds), *The Town in Ireland* (Historical Studies XIII), Belfast, 1981.

Murphy, Maura, 'The Working Classes of Nineteenth Century Cork', *Journal of the Cork Historical and Archaeological Society*, Vol. 85, 1980.

Nowlan, Kevin and T. Desmond Williams (eds), *Ireland in the War Years and After, 1939-1951*, Dublin, 1969.

O'Brien, John B., 'The Hacketts: Glimpses of Entrepeneurial Life in Cork, 1800-1870', *Journal of the Cork Historical and Archaeological Society*, Vol. 90, 1985.

O'Brien, John B., 'Merchants in Cork Before the Famine', in P. Butel and L. M. Cullen (eds), *Cities and Merchants: French and Irish Perspectives on Urban Development, 1500-1900*, Dublin, 1986.

O'Connor, Emmet, *A Labour History of Ireland 1824-1960*, Dublin, 1992.

O'Flanagan, Patrick and Cornelius G. Buttimer (eds), *Cork: History and Society - Interdisciplinary Essays on the History of an Irish County*, Dublin, 1983.

O'Halloran, Barry, 'Heineken Celebrates 10 Years in Cork', *Vintners World*, June 1993.

O'Leary, J.J., 'Developments in the Brewing Industry', *Technology Ireland*, November 1972.

O'Sullivan, William, *The Economic History of Cork City from the Earliest Times to the Act of Union*, Cork, 1937.

Reilly, A.J., *Father John Murphy: Famine Priest, 1796-1883*, Dublin, 1963.

Robins, Joseph, *The Lost Children: A Study of Charity Children in Ireland 1700-1900*, Dublin, 1980.

Roche, Michael, 'Putting Murphy's Back Together Again', *Success*, June 1982.

Rynne, Colin, *The Industrial Archaeology of Cork City and its Environs: A Pilot Survey*, Dublin, 1989.

Sprott, Duncan, *Our Lady of the Potatoes*, London, 1995.

Stratten and Stratten, *Dublin, Cork and Southern Ireland*, London, 1892.

Turpin, John, *John Hogan: Irish Neoclassical Sculptor in Rome 1800-1858*, Dublin, 1982.

Pamphlets

'Visits to the different Breweries in Ireland: The Celebrated Brewery of Sir John Arnott & Co, Cork', *Scottish Standard*, 1873.

'The Great Irish Breweries', XXVIII - Lady's Well Brewery, *The Wine Merchant and Grocer's Review*, Cork, undated.

Who Burnt Cork City?, published by the Irish Labour Party and Trade Union Congress, Dublin, 1921.

Primary Documents

Murphy Brewery Ireland Limited

A range of company papers and records dating back to 1856 is held at the brewery. It is not a complete collection and there are large gaps in each category. Nevertheless, records of some kind survive for every period in the brewery's history and they proved to be invaluable sources. The collection includes the chairman's annual reports, directors' minute books, workmen's registers, wages and salaries books, extensive tied house estate records, details on shares and shareholders, account books and assorted ledgers, manuals, note and minute books covering all aspects of the brewery's day-to-day affairs from its foundation to the present day.

Cork Archives Institute
Cork Coopers' Society Minutes and Correspondence, 1870-1950.
'Murphy Memoirs', by Katherine Donovan (née Murphy).

National Library of Ireland
'The Genealogy of the Ancient and Illustrious Family of Mary Louisa and Mary-Bridget O'Murphy of Paris'.

Cork County Library
Report of Vice-Regal Commission on Irish Railways, 1908.

Private Holdings
Genealogy of the Murphy Family compiled by Basil O'Connell, kindly lent by R.P. Murphy.

Newspapers and Periodicals
Cork Constitution
Cork Examiner
Cork Herald
Evening Echo
Irish Times
Murphy News
Murphy Times
Murphyman
New Murphy News

INDEX